My Soul Looks Back

JOURNEYS IN FAITH

Speech, Silence, Action! The Cycle of Faith
Virginia Ramey Mollenkott

Creative Dislocation—The Movement of Grace
Robert McAfee Brown

Hope Is an Open Door
Mary Luke Tobin

By Way of Response
Martin E. Marty

Ten Commandments for the Long Haul
Daniel Berrigan

God's Presence in My Life
Edward W. Bauman

Disputed Questions: On Being a Christian
Rosemary Radford Ruether

All God's Children
Tilden Edwards

A Simplicity of Faith: My Experience in Mourning
William Stringfellow

My Soul Looks Back

James H. Cone

Journeys in Faith
Robert A. Raines, Editor

ABINGDON
Nashville

MY SOUL LOOKS BACK

Copyright © 1982 by Abingdon

Library of Congress Cataloging in Publication Data

CONE, JAMES H.
  My soul looks back.
    (Journeys in faith)
      1. Cone, James H. 2. Black theology—History—20th century. 3.
    Theologians—United States—Biography.
      I. Title. II. Series.
  BX4827.C65A35   230'.044'0924   82-1708

ISBN 0-687-27616-0

Lines from "How I Got Over," by Clara Ward, are used by permission of the
Executive Publishing Administration, Chatsworth, California.

Scripture quotations are from the Revised Standard Version Common Bible,
copyrighted © 1973 by the Division of Christian Education of the National
Council of the Churches of Christ in the U.S.A., and are used by permission.

An earlier version of the material on pages 124-38 appeared in slightly different
form in "The Black Church and Marxism: What Do They Have to Say to Each
Other?" an Occasional Paper from the Institute for Democratic Socialism.

MANUFACTURED BY THE PARTHENON PRESS AT
NASHVILLE, TENNESSEE, UNITED STATES OF AMERICA

To My Wife, Sandra

How I got over
How I got over
My soul looks back
And wonders
How I got over

Contents

EDITOR'S FOREWORD...11

INTRODUCTION.. 14

1 From Bearden to Adrian.................................... 17

2 Black Theology and Black Power........................41

3 Black Theology and the Black Church............................64

4 Black Theology and Third World Theologies................. 93

5 Black Theology, Feminism, and Marxism...................... 114

NOTES.. 139

Editor's Foreword

People inside and outside the church today are engaged in a profound revisioning of the faith journey. Wanting to honor our own heritage and to be nourished by our roots, we also want to discern the signs of the kingdom now, and to move into the 1980s with a lean, biblical, ecumenical, and human faith perspective.

The *Journeys in Faith* book series is offered to facilitate this revisioning of faith. Reflecting on the social justice openings of the 1960s and the inward searching of the 1970s these books articulate a fresh integration of the faith journey for the years ahead. They are personal and social. Authors have been invited to share what has been happening to them in their faith and life in recent years, and then to focus on issues that have become primary for them in this time.

We believe that these lucidly written books will be widely used by study groups in congregations, seminaries, colleges, renewal

11

centers, orders, and denominations, as well as for personal study and reflection.

Our distinguished authors embody a diversity of experience and perspective that will provide many points of identification and enrichment for readers. As we enter into the pilgrimages shared in these books we will find resonance, encouragement, and insight for a fresh appropriation of our faith, toward personal and social transformation.

James Cone gives passionate testimony about his struggle to integrate black and Christian identities. Encouraged by a strong father to choose what he wanted to be, and urged by his hometown friends to "speak for your people," Cone proceeded to do just that. Experiencing white oppression in his home town, college, seminary, and the church, Cone struggled to get the training necessary to become a black theologian, and so to speak for his people. Anger grew in him over the years and rose up at the murder of Martin Luther King, Jr. The summer following that murder he wrote the book *Black Theology and Black Power*. It was a conversion event for him: experiencing the death of white theology and being born again into the theology of black experience. Cone came to understand a central part of his theological vocation as providing a critique of white, European-dominated theology.

He acknowledges the tension in him between striving for success as a theologian in the white, academic system, while wanting to participate in the liberation of poor blacks on the street.

Cone has a lover's quarrel with the black church, appreciating it as the community in which he heard the gospel preached and sometimes saw it lived, while criticizing its institutional self-preoccupation. Many readers will share Cone's understanding of the heart of the gospel as God's option for the poor, and his concept of the vocation of the church as agent of liberation of the poor and the victims of the world. Cone suggests that people naturally make entry into the struggle of liberation at the point where they are personally hurting the most. So it is that racism is the core issue of this book.

While espousing the unique vocation of black theology, he declares that the universalism of poor people all over the world prevents black theology from being the norm of all liberation theology. In addition he asserts that no one can articulate for another (a man for a woman, for example) what another's particular experience of oppression has been. Cone opens a window of inclusiveness by suggesting that no one can be fully liberated until every one is liberated.

There is anger in this book. Reading it is an experience of confrontation. Black readers will find nourishment from their own heritage and judgment of the black church. White readers will experience being judged by a black-eyed God, and may be encouraged to inquire what a theology of liberation for white middle-class Christians in the U.S. and Canada would look, sound, smell, taste like.

Cone's exploration of the similarities and differences between black theology and third world theologies of liberation/feminism/Marxism/ clarifies further the particular vision and vocation of black theology, and raises important questions for the shaping of a radically new social order.

Robert A. Raines

Introduction

"I believe that I will testify for what the Lord has done for me" is an often heard response in the black church. Testimony is an integral part of the black religious tradition. It is the occasion in which a believer stands before the community of faith in order to give an account of the hope that is in him or her (I Peter 3:15). The character of the testimony is always deeply personal as the believer tells his/her story of how he/she has been able to "keep the faith" in the midst of the "trials and tribulations of this unfriendly world." Through the act of storytelling, the storyteller receives a "little extra strength" to "keep on keeping on" even though the odds might be against him or her. Testimony is a spiritually liberating experience for the believer wherein he/she is empowered by God's Holy Spirit to stay on the "gospel train" until it reaches the kingdom.

Although testimony is unquestionably personal and thus primarily an individual's story, it is also a story accessible to others in the community of faith. Indeed, the purpose of testimony is not only to strengthen an individual's faith but also to build the faith of the community. There may be persons who are discouraged and do not know whether they can overcome the "principalities and powers" of this world. The testimony of a fellow believer reminds them that "though the way may be dark and the road rocky, I am a living witness that the Lord will make a way somehow." Others present may be visitors, inquiring about the possibility of joining the community of faith but not sure what value the Christian faith offers. A believer's testimony tells the story of his/her personal experience of salvation and thereby encourages hesitant persons to "step out on God's Word of promise." There are still others in the community of faith who are not tired or weary, and are not seekers of a new way but are already committed believers bearing witness to God's coming kingdom. For these persons, testimony is a regular part of their spiritual diet, reminding them that the presence of God's Holy Spirit cannot be manipulated or taken for granted.

This book is written in the tradition of black testimony. It is not an autobiography. It is rather an account of the spiritual and intellectual development of my faith—from childhood in Bearden, Arkansas, to the present. Because I am black, I am writing primarily to the black church community. It is my personal testimony of how I have struggled to keep and to live the faith of the black church. I hope that my story will help to strengthen the faith of black Christians and also encourage other blacks to share in it. The truth of my story is dependent upon the truth of the faith of the black church. Indeed it is because of my love for the black church and my commitment to its faith that I have ventured to testify.

Because I believe that the gospel is universal and thus intended for all, I have written my story in dialogue with people of other cultures and nations who also regard Jesus Christ as God's definitive and final salvation for humankind. Indeed the character and dynamic of the changes in my intellectual and spiritual development are directly related to my encounters with others, especially Christians in Asia, Africa, and Latin America, commonly called the Third World. Also the white churches of Europe and North America have presented an enormous theological challenge to my understanding of the gospel. Although I have been critical of them, the criticism was meant to be prophetic and not cynical. I firmly believe that the gospel is available to all—including white people. But the availability of the gospel is exclusively dependent upon a *conversion* experience, wherein one makes an unqualified commitment to the struggle of the poor for freedom. This *metanoia* is available to all, though not accepted by all.

1
From Bearden to Adrian

When people ask me about the decisive influences on my theological and political perspectives, my response always includes something about my mother and father, and what it meant for a black person to grow up in Bearden, Arkansas, during the 1940s and 50s. I have written briefly about Bearden and the Macedonia A.M.E. Church in other places.[1] The more I reflect on who I am, and what is important to me, the more the Bearden experience looms large in my consciousness. Is it nostalgia? It may be that, but I do not think so. I am not homesick for Bearden or even for Macedonia. The importance of Bearden is the way it enters my thinking, controlling my theoretical analysis, almost forcing me to answer questions about faith and life as found in the experience of my early years. It is as if the people of Bearden are present, around my desk as I think and write. Their voices are clear and insistent: "All right, James Hal, speak for your people."

Why do they exert such a powerful influence on my thinking, since my personal affection for them is not very strong and often ambiguous? Perhaps it is my way of searching for my roots, my reasons for being. Past, present, and future are interconnected as different moments in one's experience, and what happens in one moment invariably affects the others. I have come to realize that if I cannot make sense out of my past, then I will not be able to find my bearings in the present for the shaping of my future.

Two things happened to me in Bearden: I encountered the harsh realities of white injustice that was inflicted daily upon the black community; and I was given a faith that sustained my personhood and dignity in spite of white people's brutality. The dual reality of white injustice and black faith, as a part of the structure of life, created a tension in my being that has not been resolved. If God is good, and also all powerful, as black church folk say, why do blacks get treated so badly? That was the question that my brother Cecil and I asked at an early age, and it is still the question that creates the intellectual energy and passion for my writing today. In Bearden, my brother and I talked about the problem of suffering in the context of the Christian faith as if we had discovered something new, not knowing as we do now that such problems constitute the perennial concern of both theology and philosophy. I am sure that the existential importance of the question of suffering and faith as found in Bearden caused me to choose the ministry as my vocation.

Because of the passion with which I write and speak about white people's oppression of blacks, people sometimes think that I have had personal experience of lynching, rape, police harassment, or some other blatant expression of white brutality so common in many places in the South. But that is not the case. In fact, because of the absence of the extreme forms of oppression, the white folks of Bearden did not think of themselves as being cruel or unjust to black people. They regarded the social and political arrangements that they maintained as an expression of the natural orders of creation. White people took it for granted that blacks were supposed to address all white adults as "Mr." and "Mrs.," and they responded by calling all blacks "boy," "girl," or by their first names. If a black person was old enough and also possessed the proper deference, then he or she might have the dubious honor of being called "uncle" or "auntie." Other expressions of the black-white social arrangements involved blacks going to the back door, smiling while in the presence of whites, even when nothing was funny. I will never forget the "colored" and "white" water fountains and separate waiting rooms at the doctor's office. As I reflect back on my early years in Bearden, there is not any specific manifestation of injustice that stands out but rather the social ethos that whites created and controlled. It was an ethos that was inherently dehumanizing for black people.

Although the social and political arrangements seemed permanent and unchangeable, I could never reconcile myself to accept the social etiquette of black-white relations. In church, home, and school, I was always taught to resist oppression and injustice. The person most responsible for my deep resentment against oppression was my father. Sometimes I think that everything I feel deeply about and the passion with which I think and write are derived exclusively from him. My father was such a dominant person in the lives of his three sons that even today we still talk about his courage and integrity in difficult circumstances. The tenacity with which he defended his rights and spoke the truth, regardless of the risks, earned him much respect among some blacks and the label "crazy" among others.

My father prided himself in being able to outthink white people, to beat them at their own game. His sixth-grade education was no measure of his quick, substantial intelligence. That was why he walked and talked with such self-confidence, and also why he managed to avoid much of the dehumanizing climate of the black-white social arrangements. For example, he refused to work at the sawmills and other factories in and around Bearden because he contended that a black person could not keep his or her dignity and also work for white people. For the same reason, he refused to allow my mother to work as a maid even in the hardest times. In extreme circumstances, my mother was willing to endure the humiliation for the sake of our survival, but my father always rejected her offer. He repeatedly told his sons that if he had anything to say about it, his wife and our mother would never be allowed to subject herself to such disgrace. It was in this context that he explained why he always called my mother "Mrs. Cone" while in the presence of whites. It was his way of forcing whites to address her with dignity and not by her first name. In such situations, most whites resisted by ignoring her or by asking for her first name, which was never given. My father would not permit any white person to address my mother as "girl" or himself as "boy." These names were the ultimate insult to black people's dignity, equivalent to being called "nigger." Any white person who used those derogatory terms in the presence of my father had to be prepared for an apology or a fight.

Growing up with my father, working with him in the woods, and observing his dealings with whites and blacks had a profound affect upon my perspective about the world. He gave me the conviction that survival for black people requires constant struggle, and that no black should ever expect justice from whites. "How could they treat us justly when they do not regard us as people?" he often asked rhetorically. My father could not understand why many blacks believed what whites said to them in private conversation when their public behavior contradicted it. He contended that in private white people may say anything that is pleasing to black ears, but that means nothing. What counts is what whites say and do in public among their friends and other whites who may disagree.

Although my father seldom earned more than a thousand dollars per year and often much less, he also refused to allow white politicians during election time to place their stickers on any of his property, suggesting that he supported their candidacy. He was sometimes offered two or three hundred dollars for his support, but he always angrily declined the money. "If I vote for you," he always said, "it will not be because of money, but because I believe you are the lesser evil of the available alternatives. There is no reason for me to believe that you or any other white person will do everything you say before an election. Therefore get the hell off my property."

As a child, I was sometimes troubled about why my father refused the money from white politicians, especially when he did vote for some of them, and we did need the money badly. When I asked him about it, he replied quickly and firmly: "Don't ever let anybody buy your integrity, especially white people. Tell them that it is not for sale. Do what you do because it is right and not because of the money involved. And never let yourself be put in a position where you are dependent upon your enemies in order to survive. For God will make a way out of no way, and he will also make your enemies your footstool."

The truth of my father's saying became evident in his life. I do not ever remember worrying about our physical survival. In difficult times, when constant rain and cold or some misfortune with the truck prevented him from going into the woods to cut and haul billets, he always responded with a sense of humor. "If the Lord just help me over this little lump, then I will scale the mountain by myself."

The struggle to survive with dignity was not easy for any of the four hundred blacks of Bearden. The nearly eight hundred whites reminded them daily who was in charge of things. The assumption that "white is right" was accepted by all whites and some blacks; but it infuriated my father, and he assured me through his words and actions that such was not the case. If one is black, he or she does not have to "get back" and accept the present situation of injustice as unchangeable. That was why my father filed a lawsuit against the Bearden School Board in the early 1950s on the grounds that the white and black schools were not equal. After the Supreme Court decision of 1954, my father's suit became a case for the integration of the schools. Absolute madness seemed to enter the minds and hearts of the white folks in Bearden at the very idea of blacks and whites going to the same schools. For the first time, to my knowledge, Bearden whites began to talk about lynching Charlie Cone because he refused to take his name off of the lawsuit. We were all afraid for my father's life and urged him to leave for his own safety. My father responded: "No white person is going to make me leave my own house. Let the sons of bitches come. They may lynch me; but with this double-barrel shotgun and my pistol, some of them will die with me." Fortunately the lynch mob never came, as had been announced. Legal complications prevented the Bearden schools from being integrated until the 1960s.

The universal manifestation of courage and resistance that I saw in my father's life continues to make anything that I might achieve seem modest and sometimes insignificant. At most, what I say and do are just dim reflections of what my parents taught and lived. If they, risking livelihood and life, could make a stand against the white folks of Bearden, cannot I, protected by tenure and doctorate, at least say a few words and do a few things that represent the truth of black life?

In the context of Macedonia African Methodist Episcopal Church, resistance to white injustice was joined with faith in God's righteousness. My mother was one of the pillars of Macedonia, and a firm believer in God's justice. Since my father joined the church because of the pressure that my mother applied before their marriage, he sometimes had to be reminded by her that God alone is the supreme judge of all things. There were times when he relied exclusively upon his physical and mental resources as if there was no spiritual power at work in the world. In such times, my mother was quick to silence him as his language moved toward disrespect for the mystery of God's presence in the world in the midst of oppression.

The spirituality that my mother embodied was typical of black Christians in Bearden, especially Macedonia. It was not until my graduate school days that I heard many professors and students using the black church as a prime example regarding the truth of the Marxist critique of religion. The force of the Marxist logic seemed to fit perfectly the white churches in Bearden but did not appear to apply to the true essence of black religion as I had encountered it. I do not ever remember any black church person in Bearden using religion to cover up oppression or as an escape from the harsh realities of life.

Religion was rather the source of identity and survival, on the one hand, and the source of empowerment in the struggle for freedom on the other.

As a source of identity and survival, the faith of the church was that factor which sustained the people when everything else failed. God was that reality to which the people turned for identity and worth because the existing social, political, and economic structures said that they were nobody. How were they to know that they were somebody when their humanity was not recognized by the existing arrangement, and when it appeared that they were powerless to do anything about it? It is in this context that the origin of black religion must be analyzed and interpreted, especially in Bearden, Arkansas. After being treated as things for six days of the week, black folk went to church on Sunday in order to affirm and experience another definition of their humanity. In the eyes of the Almighty, they were children of God whose future was not defined by the white structures that humiliated them. That was why they called each other Mr. and Mrs. or brother and sister. The value structures in the society were completely reversed in the church. The last became first in that the janitor became the chairman of the Steward Board and the maid became the president of Stewardess Board Number One. Everybody became somebody, and there were no second-class people at Macedonia.

In their struggle to affirm their dignity and also survive, there were many times when that possibility seemed to vanish and the future seemed closed. The experience of despair often happened at a personal level in response to the death of a loved one. Or it could happen as the community tried to achieve a measure of justice in white society. But in either case, when the people of Macedonia had their backs up against the wall and all human resources appeared exhausted, they did not hesitate to turn to the Lord in prayer.

> When you are in trouble, burdened with care,
> And know not what to do;

Fear ye not to call His name
And He will fix it for you.

For some Marxists and other leftists who do not know existentially the black religious experience, the survival and identity emphasis of black religion will surely validate their claim that it is an opiate. There are of course many black churches that are vulnerable to the Marxist critique. But I would claim that to apply the label of opiate to black religion in Bearden during my early years is to be doctrinaire and superficial, neglecting to probe the depths of the black experience that gave birth to the church. (In chapter 5, I will discuss Marxism's relation to the black church in greater detail.)

Furthermore, labeling religion a mere pain-killer ignores the black church as the source, not only of identity and survival, but of the sociopolitical struggle for liberation. During my childhood, every fight for justice and civil rights was initiated in and led by the church. The leader was usually the minister or some other self-employed black person. Because there were very few black people who were not dependent upon whites for a livelihood, the burden of leadership fell upon the preacher whose salary was paid by his congregation. Seeing so many courageous ministers leading the struggle for justice in the name of the gospel, and also seeing the support of church people, undoubtedly had much to do with why I chose the ministry as my vocation, and also why I chose liberation as the central theme of my perspective in black theology. How could I write about black theology and overlook the theme of liberation in the gospel preached at Macedonia and in black church history? It would be like writing about God of the Old Testament and overlooking the Exodus or of the New Testament and failing to mention the cross and the resurrection of Jesus, and what they mean for people struggling for freedom. (Of course European and North American churches and their theologians have been doing that for centuries, so we must recognize that anything is possible in biblical interpretation.)

In 1954, I graduated from high school and entered Shorter, a small two-year unaccredited college of the African Methodist Episcopal Church in North Little Rock, Arkansas. Later I transferred to Philander Smith, a slightly larger but accredited Methodist college in Little Rock. Both colleges opened up a new world for me. Leaving Bearden and going eighty miles to the "big city" of Little Rock was like going to another country. The problem of the relation between faith and justice could be viewed from a larger perspective. I began to read and hear about Martin Luther King, Jr., and the Montgomery bus boycott, and I experienced firsthand the 1957 integration crisis at Central High School. I was a student at Philander not very far from Central when Daisy Bates masterminded the integration of nine black students at the largest white high school in Little Rock.[2] One of the nine students, Elizabeth Eckford, was a member of my brother's church.

Those were very rough and tense days. Once again the true nature of American democracy and white religion was revealed, and no amount of clever theological analysis could make black people think that the whites who harassed those nine black children were also Christians. Our certainty about the rightness of integration left no room for debate about the justice of the case or the righteousness of God. All blacks seemed to think that God was on our side and against the satanic force of white supremacy. We did not need approval of white theologians and preachers to know that whites were in the wrong both morally and legally. Who can read the Bible or the 1954 Supreme Court decision and conclude otherwise? Only racist white people!

Because white church people seemed not to know the obvious (i.e., that justice was God's will), many blacks thought that they were ignorant regarding spiritual and biblical matters and thus needed to be converted. Black people have always assumed that one needed more than "book knowledge" in order to know and to do God's will. In black religion, knowledge of right and wrong was derived from people's encounter with and conversion by the Holy Spirit. Since whites persisted in their wrongdoings regarding racism, despite their university training or formal church affiliation, black Christians assumed that they had not been converted.

I must admit that I often made similar assumptions. But I also thought that white people's wrongdoings toward blacks were due to a lack of actual knowledge of what the Bible said and the absence of a black confrontation of them with the truth of the gospel. Once confronted with the gospel and the demands that it lays upon all Christians, then whites would cease their racism, I thought, because their Christian identity was more important to them than their humiliation of blacks. I really wanted to believe that whites desired to do the right thing, because it was the *Christian* thing to do. How could anyone claim an identity with Jesus and be for injustice? Because the behavior of whites blatantly contradicted the gospel, and because I thought that whites did such cruel things out of ignorance, I decided that I would inform them when the next appropriate occasion occurred.

On one occasion, while riding a public bus, I sat down next to an elderly, churchly looking white woman who seemed so serious and pious. (The buses were legally segregated, but my brother and I never observed that rule.) She quickly got up, uttering angry expletives at me. I went over to her, with a smile on my face so as to calm her down. I said: "Madam, you look like a Christian, and that was why I sat down by you. How could you say the things you said to me when Jesus said that what you do to the least you do to him?" "You are not Jesus," she replied with hate and violence in her eyes. "Get the hell out of my face, you nigger!" From this and similar events, I began to realize that even if people know the truth, they will not necessarily do it. I also began to realize that religion did not automatically make people sensitive to human pain and suffering. Perhaps black church people were right. What white people needed was a conversion experience. But how and when would whites be converted? While black church people left such matters in the hands of the Holy Spirit, I wanted to explore the complexity of this problem more deeply through a study of theology and history.

As I observed white churches' response to the crisis at Central High School and related problems of racism, I became more confused about the relationship between the Christian gospel and social justice. I did not know where to turn for an analysis of this theological issue. White churches, almost without exception, were adamant in rejecting integration in churches, schools, and social gatherings. Black churches, however, were equally determined on the other side of the issue. How could both black and white churches be Christian if they took opposite stands and both claimed Christ and the Bible as the basis of their views? The issues involved seemed to me to be as important theologically as those that spurred the Protestant Reformation in Europe. Therefore, I began to think that what Richard Allen, the founder of the AME Church, did during the late eighteenth and early nineteenth centuries was as revolutionary as what Martin Luther did in the sixteenth century. But because I was so limited in what I knew about theology and the history of both black and white churches, I had to wait before I could analyze more clearly what I felt in the depths of my being. I had a lot of hunches about theology and its relation to social existence but no social or theological framework in which to pursue my concerns. I had not read Marx, Rauschenbusch, or the sociologists of knowledge.

The existential need to analyze the contradictions in the black experience created in me a ceaseless intellectual curiosity. I wanted to read everything related to human problems that I could get my hands on. Shorter and Philander Smith provided an excellent educational context for the pursuit of my concerns. They disclosed a new world of knowledge to me. These two small black colleges took me as I was, with few intellectual resources, and made me believe that I could think. There was no way that I could have left Ouachita County Training School in Bearden for any major white college or university. I was neither emotionally nor intellectually ready for that. There is no question in my mind whatsoever that I am a professor of theology at a major seminary today because of the black church and its schools. Black teachers at my high school, along with the church and home, taught me that I was somebody with the warmth of their love and their constant affirmation of my personhood. But at Shorter and Philander, I was introduced to a world of scholarship with philosophers, historians, and theologians. I began to read about Socrates and Plato, Aquinas and Luther, Kant and Hegel. The most interesting of all my subjects was "Negro history," as it was called in those days. I had been introduced briefly to black history in my high school, but college enabled me to explore the subject more deeply.

The more I read about black history, the more I became proud that I was black. Growing up with proud parents, attending black schools, and being a minister in a black church did much to make me proud of my blackness. But without a knowledge of one's past, such things cannot sustain one's sense of worth in a racist society. A person without a past is a person without an identity. And the absence of an identity is very serious, because without self-knowledge others can make you become what they desire. When that insight was revealed to me, I also realized why whites omitted black people's contributions to humankind in their writing and teaching and in both secular and religious subjects. That was and is their way of making us think that we are nothing. To be nothing means that you have done nothing in history worthwhile. To do nothing means that you cannot think. Therefore others must think for you and organize the society without your participation in the organization.

As I reflected on this issue, the more complex it became. I needed more help with the actual content of black history. For the first time, I began to read Frederick Douglass, Booker T. Washington, W. E. B. DuBois, and Carter G. Woodson. Reading black thinkers, mostly historians, I encountered the various ways that black people have struggled against white racism. I learned that black people have never been as passive as whites had suggested in their history books. Therefore my contemporary rebellious spirit had its roots in earlier black generations. This knowledge was quite liberating.

Although black history was the most interesting subject, history as a discipline was not nearly as interesting as were religion and philosophy. I was not interested in the mere study of the past as a body of information and facts. Rather, I was interested in a study of the past in order to analyze the present, so that black people would know how to make a different future. That was why I decided to major in religion and philosophy.

With my interest in oral skills, I enjoyed not only preaching, but also lively debates inside and outside the classroom. I really liked philosophy because of the technical skills in the logic required to win an argument. Unfortunately I did not write much in college, and that weakness almost caused my failure in graduate school. In college, church, home, and other aspects of black life, oral skills were the key to success. Because I was fairly good at it, I did well in my classes.

But when I left Little Rock for Evanston, Illinois, to attend Garrett Biblical Institute (now Garrett-Evangelical Theological Seminary) in 1958, I was hardly ready for the emotional and intellectual challenge that awaited me. My brother and I went to Evanston to attend Garrett together, and neither of us will ever forget the devastating experiences that happened to us. Most of these unpleasant and humiliating experiences were due to our naïveté. We mistakenly believed that blacks were really free "up North." This was partly due to the stories that our Northern relatives had told us Southern blacks so as to make us feel bad and themselves good. Unfortunately I believed them. But it did not take more than one day before the myth was broken, and I was rudely awakened to the fact that white America is the same everywhere. The only difference is a matter of social and political taste.

My first awakening occurred when I decided to go for a haircut at a white barber shop, naïvely thinking that everybody went there or places like it. Did not freedom mean that a person could go to any public place for service, and were not Northern cities free for all people? When I walked into that barber shop I thought I noticed expressions of surprise on the white faces inside. Then as soon as I sat down, one of the barbers came over to me and said: "We don't cut niggers' hair in this place." "Excuse me," I said, "but I am not a nigger. It appears that you and your customers are the niggers." I quickly departed, not knowing how emotionally to assimilate the experience. I have never really quite gotten over that experience. It was not that I blamed the whites in that barber shop. Rather I blamed myself for being so naïve, so stupid as to believe that whites in Evanston and Chicago would be much different from whites in Little Rock and Bearden. I was so angry with myself and so embarrassed by my own stupidity that I did not tell anybody about it, not even my brother, until much later.

Similar revealing experiences happened to me at Garrett. Lest I am misunderstood, I want to emphasize that Garrett was not any worse for blacks than any of the other white seminaries of that time. In fact I really believe that it was more responsive to the needs of blacks than many seminaries like it. The problem was my naïveté. Garrett was not only "up North," but was a *Christian* institution. One would think that, having experienced the contradiction of faith and injustice in the white churches of Arkansas, and having had a humiliating experience in an Evanston barber shop, only a few blocks from Garrett, I would have been ready for a few contradictions at Garrett as well. After all the disappointments that I had experienced with so-called white Christians, and in view of my knowledge of similar things happening to black people in American history, how could I have been so unsuspecting?

My expectation of fairness raises the larger question of why many black people continue to believe that they will receive justice from whites when there is so little in our history to warrant it. What is the source of our optimism despite white hypocrisy and deception? Even a casual reading of black history in the United States shows that many black people really expected freedom after the Revolutionary War, the war of 1812, the Civil War, and World Wars I and II. In fact, this spirit of black optimism was partly the philosophical foundation of the civil rights movement of the 1960s. Although there are also some significant exceptions to the black faith in white fairness, the dominant theme in black life appears to be the belief that one day whites will do right. Is black religion the source of that hope? Or is it black people's mental internalization of the values of their oppressors? Both are probably involved along with other factors.

Regardless of the causes of my expectation to find justice at Garrett, very little was found there. Many professors treated black students as if they were dumb. One professor was well known for the racist jokes that he told regularly in his classes. The irony was that he taught Christian ethics. Within the context of Garrett's hostile, strange, and white environment, I barely made all C's my first quarter. The drop from being an A student in college to a C student in seminary was very humiliating. And when I went to talk to my professors about my grades, they looked at me with amazement. All contended that I deserved less, and that it was out of their Christian spirit that I received the grades I did. Also all said in their own way that they did not expect blacks to do any better than C.

With my professors thinking that I was only average, regardless of my college grades at Shorter and Philander, I was faced with an enormous challenge. I had discussed this matter earlier with five or six other black students, and the older ones assured the newcomers that white professors seldom gave black students anything higher than a C. But it was not until three professors said it to my face that the gravity of the matter began to sink in.

Because my experience at Garrett was so typical of white graduate schools of that time (and even today), one wonders why any black students stayed long enough to even get a degree. This problem continues to be intensified because most white administrators, professors, and students do not know what blacks are talking about when we speak of an ethos of racism. It is as if whites have been socially conditioned to be racist and thus dehumanizing to blacks for so long that they now do not even recognize it any longer. This was my feeling at Garrett, and I felt that there was little that I could do to change the attitudes of whites at Garrett regarding their prejudices about blacks.

Although I did not go to Garrett with the intention of getting a Ph.D. degree, I was determined to make liars of my professors regarding my intellectual ability, even with them being the judges. I realized that I could not possibly change their general perceptions of black students, but I was determined to change their particular perception of me as a C student. My father's spirit of resistance began to rise in me as they tried to encourage me to be contented with my "black inferiority." As I reflected upon what they had said to me, I said to myself: "I am going to show all of you white professors that I am not stupid. I am going to make you eat those words."

I should point out that this early encounter with professors at Garrett was not the crisis event that led me to think about the idea of black theology. That later event was only indirectly related to my educational experience at Garrett. At this particular time, my comments merely expressed my determination to make better grades than C's. During the second quarter, I decided to take only two courses, the minimum of registration as a full-time student. I began a disciplined program of study and soon found out that my chief difficulty was with writing term papers. Despite my writing deficiency and the skepticism of my teachers regarding my intellectual ability, I managed to get two B's, a real boost for my self-confidence. I never expected to become an A student overnight. I knew that it would take several quarters, and two B's were merely one step toward my goal.

As I analyzed my situation, I realized that what I needed to do was to enlarge my verbal skills beyond those of speech; I must develop the technical skills of writing term papers. But in order to do that, I needed to know more about the structure of the English language. I purchased a ninth-grade English text and began an independent program of learning how to write. I was embarrassed when I faced the reality that I did not know how to write. But my pride in proving my professors wrong was more important than the personal embarrassment of studying a ninth-grade English text.

In addition to studying the structure of the English language, I also began to read writers in history, literature, and sociology. I observed closely not only the content of what they said but also the way they said it. I began to realize that being an effective writer was similar to being an effective speaker. The style was nearly as important as the content. What difference does it make to write or speak the truth if it is put in a style that is boring or unclear? As a black preacher and pastor, I learned early that effective delivery was important in eliciting response from the audience. Is not the same true for writing? I knew that if I were going to achieve any degree of success as a writer in graduate school, I had to consider the people to whom I was writing, and the form in which they expected good writing to appear.

Although I was still struggling with my writing, I had become a straight A student by the time I reached my senior year. When I took the comprehensive exams for the bachelor of divinity (now master of divinity) degree, I passed with distinction. Later I was awarded the systematic theology prize for being the best student in that area. With these academic accomplishments, I felt that I had shown my professors that their early evaluation of my intellectual ability was totally wrong. I knew now that I could be whatever I chose, as my father had always told me.

It was during my senior year that I decided to apply for the program leading to the Ph.D. degree. Two factors influenced my decisions. (1) Although I had planned to return to Arkansas to pastor an AME church, there was no church available for me. (2) William Hordern and Philip S. Watson, both professors of systematic theology, took an interest in me and urged me to stay on for the Ph.D. degree. After I had passed the comprehensive exams with distinction, William Hordern, who was on the committee, came to me later and asked, "You are applying for the Ph.D. program, are you not?" I responded with surprise: "No, I had not thought about it. Do you think that I could do it?" "What do you mean?" he quickly responded. "You are one of the best students I have ever taught in systematic theology. Of course you can do it." "Will you be my advisor?" I asked. "Of course," he said.

After that conversation with Hordern, one of the most respected teachers at Garrett, I was truly excited. As a black student who had been told about my educational limitations by several Garrett professors, to receive such encouragement from Hordern was what I needed in order to take the risk of doing the Ph.D. degree. When I went to talk with Philip Watson about it, he was equally encouraging and also offered to work with Hordern as my advisor. This was almost too good to be true. After talking this matter over with my first wife, Rose, I decided that I had little to lose and everything to gain by trying what no other black student had done before me.

Since Garrett offered me no scholarship, I had to work part-time as a janitor and painter, labor twelve hours per week for a white family who owned the garage apartment where we lived, and also serve as an assistant pastor at Woodlawn AME Church in Chicago. Working many hours, however, was not my major difficulty. Despite Hordern's and Watson's encouragement, I had to confront racism embedded in the educational structures at Garrett and often blatantly expressed in the attitude of several professors and administrators. To my knowledge, confirmed by others, Garrett had never had a black Ph.D. student. When I went to inquire about the M.A. and Ph.D. program at Garrett-Northwestern, the acting graduate advisor at Garrett, who was also professor of Christian ethics, looked at me as if I were insane. "You are not going to apply for the M.A. and Ph.D. program are you?" he asked. "Yes, that is my intention," I responded. "Well, I will inform you that you will not be accepted. You don't have a chance. In fact, there are several straight-A white students from Yale and Harvard whom we are rejecting. Now what chance do you think you have?"

After hearing that, I was depressed, not knowing what to do. I returned to Hordern and told him what had been told to me. He became angry, and his response was emphatic: "Jim, you go right ahead and apply, and if you are not accepted, then I will quit." That was the first time that any white person ever put himself on the line for me. I relaxed, because I knew that Garrett would not let one of their best and most respected scholars depart over a matter such as this. I also realized later that the graduate advisor was acting on his own prejudice and not implementing stated academic policy. His comments about Yale and Harvard students were meant to intimidate me and were actually not true. Many Garrett students with averages much lower than mine were accepted for the M.A. and Ph.D. program. During my doctoral work I never received any form of financial assistance from Garrett, except a permission for me to borrow about a thousand dollars from the Federal government. Even when I requested permission to borrow money from the government, I was insulted by a chief administrator, because he claimed that I was not really on the Ph.D. program. He told me that if I were on the doctoral program, I would have no financial problems, because all Garrett Ph.D. students were automatically given major scholarships. For a moment I thought my financial problems would be solved but I also noticed a typical white rudeness as he picked up the telephone to call the graduate advisor to verify whether I was telling the truth. "Is Jim Cone on the doctoral program?" he asked. Apparently he was given an affirmative answer, and he turned to me and said: "I will okay your permission for a Federal loan." I desperately wanted to ask him about his earlier contention that all doctoral students are given scholarships. But I let it pass because I was too close to finishing to risk being dismissed for insubordination. I merely said to myself that we would meet again in a different situation and with better odds in my favor. There was no way for me to win a battle with him at that time.

The M.A. and Ph.D. programs were exciting but very difficult. Although I managed to make all A's, I still continued to encounter difficulties in writing. I was worried about writing an M.A. thesis and a Ph.D. dissertation in a style acceptable to my professors. After I completed the M.A. thesis, my concern was intensified. My advisors were patient and offered much assistance. It was also during this time that I met Lester B. Scherer, a white Ph.D. student in church history. We became very good friends, and he demonstrated to me some excellent points about how to write. He took the mystery out of writing and showed me that anyone can be a good writer if he has something to say and practices saying it. After much practice, I began to develop more confidence in my writing skills.

However, my most difficult problem in graduate school was not learning how to write but rather learning how to stay in school during the peak of the civil rights movement. How could I write papers about the Barth-Brunner debates on natural theology while black people were being denied the right to vote? Many of my black classmates, including my brother, were deeply engaged in the civil rights struggle. Some blacks asked me how I could stay in the library, reading ancient documents about Nicaea and Chalcedon, while blacks were fighting for their freedom in the streets. These were tough questions. While I am confident now that I made an appropriate decision for my vocational commitment, I was not certain at the time that I made the right decision. All I knew then was that I had an intellectual craving to do theology and to relate it to black people's struggle for justice.

How was I going to relate systematic theology to black people's fight for freedom in society? That was one of my chief questions. Answering that question was not easy, because there were no scholarly models for me to follow. Christian ethics was the natural link for the connection of the problem of racism with systematic theology, but the only professor in that area was the most blatant racist at Garrett. In the only course I took from him, which was required, I received a C and felt myself lucky. I was not about to subject myself to his racist insults any more than absolutely necessary. The only option, I felt, was to struggle with the discipline of systematic theology under the guidance of two people who, at least, were not racist in their personal dealings with me.

It is revealing to note that during my nearly six years of residence at Garrett-Northwestern, not one text written by a black person was ever used as a required reading for a class. The absence of a black scholar on the reading list had profound effects upon the self-esteem of black students. If no black was intellectually worthy to be included on the reading list, it meant that black people had nothing to say worthwhile regarding the gospel of Jesus. Was this not the opinion of white slaveholders and their supporters? What, then, was the difference between the slaveholders and the professors at Garrett? Now I realized that there were some important differences, but what surprised me were the many similarities.

Equally problematic for my stay at Garrett was the absence of the discussion of racism as a *theological* problem. For a black person who was born in the South and whose church came into being because of racism, the failure to discuss it as a central problem in theology appeared strange and racist to me. It seemed that the central problems in American theology were imported from Europe, especially Germany. Anyone who could speak German and who studied under one of the famous European theologians was always regarded as smarter than those who did not receive such academic privileges. Even though the civil rights movement was the hottest news item in America and had been identified by most as the critical problem facing the churches of the 1960s, no theologians defined the problem as a central issue in theology. Most North American theologians identified their task as keeping up with the problems defined by European theologians.

In one class I decided to make the connection between racism and theology in a highly provocative manner, by saying to one of my professors that he was a racist, since he could easily talk about the injustice that Roman Catholics inflicted on Protestants in the sixteenth century, but failed to say a word against white Christians (Protestants and Catholics) who openly support black suffering in the U.S. today. There was complete silence in the classroom, followed by a sudden outburst of anger from the professor: "That's simply not true! Class dismissed!"

After that event, I realized that Garrett would not be the best context for expressing my deepest feelings about racism, if I expected to get a Ph.D. degree from that institution. That was why I did not raise the racism issue as a theological problem and also why I decided to write a dissertation on Karl Barth's anthropology rather than some issue in the black community.

Before completing my doctoral dissertation, I accepted a teaching position at Philander Smith College in January 1964. Hearing so many stories about people who completed everything *except* the dissertation, I was determined not to let that happen to me. Through long hours of work, the patience of students, and the encouragement of my advisors, I completed my dissertation during the summer, defended it successfully in the fall, and participated in the graduation exercises in the spring of 1965.

I will never forget the graduation event. There were five students receiving the Ph.D. degree in religion at Garrett-Northwestern that year and, with a sense of pride in my achievement I stood in the middle, two others on each side. I waited for the Garrett professor who told racist jokes and who said that I would never be accepted on the Ph.D. program. He congratulated the first two doctoral students, shaking their hands; then he skipped me as I extended my hand, and went to the next two, congratulating them for their outstanding achievement. I could not believe that he could continue to be so obvious with his racism. But I smiled and said to myself: "Racism runs deep even among seminary professors." Getting a Ph.D. degree was a milestone. It was something my Bearden experience had never taught me about, and few people seemed to understand what I was doing in school for so long. To complete this degree, therefore, made me one of the happiest persons in the world, and I did not care whether white folks shook my hand or not. Even though I did not know what the future was for me, I felt that the racist professor had not seen or heard the last of me.

I returned to Philander Smith with added enthusiasm. But what did Barth, Tillich, and Brunner have to do with young black girls and boys coming from the cotton fields of Arkansas, Tennessee, and Mississippi seeking to make a new future for themselves? This was *the* major question for me. And it was further intensified by the civil rights struggle. The contradiction between theology as a discipline and the struggle for black freedom in the streets was experienced at the deepest level of my being. How was I going to resolve it? I had spent six years studying theology, and now I found it irrelevant to the things that mattered most to me. I tried my hand at writing articles about Barth and Feuerbach and the death-of-God theology for publication. They were rejected, and rightly so, because my heart was not in them. I did not know what to do. Was I going to be one of those scholars who received a Ph.D. but was never heard of afterward? Was I going to teach and write about things completely unrelated to problems in the black community? I was in an intellectual quandary. On the one hand, I was involved existentially with the civil rights movement, but on the other, I did not know how to relate theology to the black struggle for justice.

In 1964 Joseph Washington published his well-known book, *Black Religion*,[3] which many blacks regarded as combining poor scholarship and bad taste. But whites praised the book, apparently because Washington claimed that black religion was unchristian in that it identified the gospel with the struggle for justice in society. The gospel, he claimed, has to do with faith and the creeds of the church, and not with justice and the civil rights movement. Knowing that I had a Ph.D. in theology and my involvement in the civil rights movement, several black preachers and teachers asked me to write a response to Washington's critique of the black church. Existentially I was against Washington, but intellectually I did not know at the time how to refute him. If I accepted the definition of Christianity as taught in graduate school, then Washington had a strong case. Although I did not like his conclusions anymore than any black person, they seemed logical, given his premises. In order for me to challenge Washington, I had to challenge the entire white theological establishment, and I was not ready to do that. But the problems he raised stayed on my mind constantly, and I knew that I would have to challenge his identity of the Christian faith with the faith of white churches. The problem was how to do it on theological grounds and in a manner consistent with my intellectual training in theology.

In 1966 I left Philander Smith because the administration

made it clear to me that my departure would be welcome. It appeared that I was not properly submissive to the white people who controlled the board of trustees. I failed to grin when I was supposed to, and that was resented by the "powers that be" in the administration and on the board. As I observed Philander Smith, the teachers and students were good and committed to excellence in education. But the white members of the board had other concerns. They were unquestionably committed to keeping Philander Smith mediocre so that it would not in any way compete with another Methodist institution, Hendrix College, in Conway, Arkansas, only about thirty miles from Little Rock. Therefore many young black professors were urged to leave, and some administrators were dismissed when they became too interested in the best education for black students. When one compares the financial resources of Philander Smith with those of Hendrix, one can only conclude that the difference is racism. I assumed that white people would support Hendrix over Philander, but I did think that they would not interfere with committed teachers. I had also assumed that their old-time racism was a thing of the past. But on both counts, I was completely wrong.

I concluded that if I was going to teach at a white-controlled school, the control might as well be obvious. That was when I left Philander Smith to teach at Adrian College in Adrian, Michigan.

2
Black Theology and Black Power

It was not until I moved to Adrian that a clear outline of a black theology began to emerge in my theological consciousness. Although I had thought about it as early as my college days at Shorter and Philander Smith, I had no name to specify my concern and no intellectual structure in which to articulate it. Even during my six years at Garrett-Northwestern and my involvement in the civil rights movement, I did not find a name or a theoretical frame in which to say what I felt. Furthermore, the intellectual demands of graduate school did not leave me much time for any reflection except the kind needed to complete the degree. At Philander Smith, I was so involved in the politics of the school and the various adjustments of being a new teacher that I had almost no time left for independent thinking. While the idea of black theology was still in the process of development, a name for it eluded my grasp as did the theory for expressing it.

It is ironic and still a bit mysterious to me that Adrian became the place for me to write my first essay on black theology. Adrian had fewer than seventy-five blacks in a city of twenty-five thousand and only about ten in a college student population of nearly twelve hundred. I was thus removed from the community that had defined my being and from which I had never before been separated. How was it possible for me to formulate the idea of a black theology in such a place as that?

There are many factors involved in the answer to that question, some of which are too complex and others too vague to mention here. What is clear is that Adrian provided me with time for reflection which I had never had before. There was no need for me to make an emotional investment in Adrian College as I had done at Philander Smith. Neither did I have the academic pressure experienced at Garrett-Northwestern. All I had to do was to teach a few basic courses in religion and theology to mostly white students who were eager to learn information about the world but not interested in changing it. I disturbed them with my ideas only rarely, and thus spent most of my time reading and thinking about how to formulate the theological meaning of black people's commitment to political and social justice.

I felt so alone and isolated in Adrian, because there was no black person I could talk to about my deepest feelings. Lester Scherer was a good friend who shared my emotional hurts, which were increasingly more severe as I tried to make sense out of the gospel and the black struggle for justice. But he was white and not black, and that fact limited his capacity to participate in my pain and my struggle to overcome it. My salvation was found in black music (spirituals, gospels, blues, and jazz) combined with a disciplined program of reading black literature and other writers concerned about human suffering. I immersed myself in the writings of Baldwin, Wright, Fanon, Camus, Sartre, and Ellison as well as the new black writers emerging from the context of the Black Power movement. When I compared Baldwin, Wright, Ellison, and LeRoi Jones (now Amiri Baraka) with Barth, Tillich, Brunner, and Reinhold Niebuhr, I concluded that I was in the wrong field. How could I continue to allow my intellectual life to be consumed by the theological problems defined by people who had enslaved my grandparents? Since there was nothing in Euro-American theology that spoke directly to slavery, colonization, and poverty, why should I let white theologians tell me what the gospel is?

Existentially, my commitment to black people's struggle for freedom was unshakable, and the longer I lived in Adrian the firmer that commitment became. There was no doubt in my mind that the black struggle for freedom was right, both morally and legally. It did not matter to me what white preachers and politicians said about "law and order" and "Christian love." But rejecting them did not produce a theological structure in which to express logically what I felt existentially. In fact, theology seemed irrelevant to black life and suffering. So I quit reading it and devoted myself to reading secular writers, mainly blacks, who at least did not use religion to cover up human suffering.

The apparent irrelevance of theology created a vocational crisis in me, and I did not know what to do about my future as a theologian. I began to develop an intense dislike for theology because it avoided the really hard problems of life with its talk about revelation, God, Jesus, and the Holy Spirit. When the murderers of humanity seize control of the public meaning of the Christian faith, it is time to seek new ways of expressing the truth of the gospel. It was this conviction that led me to consider returning to Chicago for a Ph.D. in literature. I discussed the possibility of my return to graduate school with Nathan Scott, Jr., who was then teaching theology and literature at the University of Chicago. It was then the summer of 1967, and before I could make the necessary arrangements for my return, forty-three people were killed in the Detroit riot. Similar events occurred that summer in many other American cities. There was no time for me to return to graduate school. I had to say something now about God and black people's struggle for freedom. But what could I say?

The challenge to say something about God and the black liberation struggle was enhanced as I read and heard the comments of white theologians and preachers who condemned black violence but said nothing about the structural white violence that created it. They quoted to blacks Jesus' sayings about "love your enemy" and "turn the other cheek" but ignored their application to themselves. I was so furious that I could hardly contain my rage. The very sight of white people made me want to vomit. "Who are they," I said, "to tell us blacks about Christian ethics?" In view of white people's history of violence against humankind, how can their preachers and theologians dare to speak to the victims about love and nonviolence? My rage was intensified because most whites seemed not to recognize the contradictions that were so obvious to black people.

Although I was isolated in Adrian, I began to read about an ad hoc National Committee of Negro Churchmen (now the National Conference of Black Churchmen) who are still best known for their support of Black Power with their July 1966 statement in the *New York Times*.[1] I shouted for joy when I read their statement because it showed that prophetic voices were still present in the black church. I wanted to join their group but had no way of making myself known to them. I have never thought of myself as a public leader but only as a scholar-theologian actively concerned about the elimination of human suffering.

It was not until Ronald Goetz (a classmate during my student years at Garrett) invited me in February 1968 to lecture at Elmhurst College, where he was teaching, that I sat down to write my first essay entitled "Christianity and Black Power." I will never forget the event of writing that essay. It seemed that both my Christian and black identity was at stake. My first priority was my black identity, and I was not going to sacrifice it for the sake of a white interpretation of the gospel that I had learned at Garrett. If Christ was not to be found in black people's struggle for freedom, if he were not found in the ghettos with rat-bitten black children, if he were in rich white churches and their seminaries, then I wanted no part of him. The issue for me was not whether Black Power could be adjusted to meet the terms of a white Christ, but whether the biblical Christ is to be limited to the prejudiced interpretations of white scholars. I was determined to set down on paper what I felt in my heart.

I decided to write a brief manifesto identifying Black Power with the gospel of Jesus. I knew that a persuasive presentation of that thesis would cause the theological hairs on the heads of white theologians and preachers to stand up straight. From Barth and others I knew all about the ideological dangers of my procedure. Identifying the gospel with historico-political movements was anathema to anyone who bases his theology on divine revelation. But I purposely intended to be provocative in much the same way that Barth was when he rebelled against liberal theology. As Barth had turned liberal theology up-side-down, I wanted to turn him right-side-up with a focus on the black struggle in particular and oppressed people generally. No longer would I allow an appeal to divine revelation to camouflage God's identification with the human fight for justice.

I was angry not with Barth but only with European and North American Barthians who used him to justify doing nothing about the struggle for justice. I have always thought that Barth was closer to me than to them. But whether I was right or wrong about where Barth would stand on the matter, the truth was that I no longer was going to allow privileged white theologians to tell me how to do theology. The writing of the essay provided the occasion for me to declare my liberation from the bondage of white theology. I knew that they would not like what I was saying, including many of my former teachers at Garrett. But that did not matter since I was not writing for their approval. I was writing for black people, and only they could stand in judgment of what I was saying.

As I reflect, I must say that I do not know how Lester Scherer endured my rage against the white community, and from which I would not let him exclude himself. He read my essay, and we discussed it many times. It was difficult for us to remain close friends and also speak honestly about the sensitive issues in my essay. We succeeded because we both made a commitment to fight as best we could against the structures that separated us.

Following the February 1968 Elmhurst lecture, I attended the organizing meeting of the Black Methodists for Church

Renewal in Cincinnati, Ohio, during the same month. For the first time, I met Stokely Carmichael and C. Eric Lincoln. Negail Riley of the Methodist Church's Board of Global ministries introduced me to Lincoln and also suggested that he should read my essay "Christanity and Black Power." Lincoln read it immediately and discussed it with me until about 3:00 A.M. He suggested some revisions, but assured me that I had made a creative theological statement. His words of encouragement gave me confidence that what I had written was worth saying and had intellectual credibility.[2]

Later, through Lincoln's influence, I was invited to lecture at Colgate Rochester Divinity School in the spring of 1968. After my lecture, I was offered a teaching post but not in systematic theology. I declined the offer, because I was committed now to making sense out of systematic theology. A position in systematics was available, but apparently the administration and faculty were not sure that I was intellectually capable of filling it. In order to explore this possibility further, I was invited to present four lectures in the fall of 1968 as a theological fellow. I accepted because it gave me an opportunity to analyze more deeply the relation between Christianity and Black Power.

Martin Luther King, Jr.'s assassination (April 4, 1968) marked a turning point in the political consciousness of many black Americans regarding nonviolence as a method for social change and as an expression of Christian love. Because of King's commitment to nonviolence and thus rejection of Black Power, many blacks were cautious in their public acceptance of Black Power in that it implied a rejection of Martin King. But after he was killed by white violence, Black Power seemed not only a logical but a necessary choice for the black community.

Although I had already embraced Black Power before King's murder, that event intensified my conviction and made me more determined to write an extended essay equating Black Power with the Christian gospel. By the summer of that year, I had so much anger pent up in me that I had to let it out or be destroyed by it. The cause of my anger was not merely my reaction to the murder of Martin King. Neither was it due simply to the death of Malcolm X or the killing of so many blacks in the cities. My anger stretched back to the slave ships, the auction block, and the lynchings. But even more important were my personal encounters with racism in Bearden, Little Rock, Evanston, and Adrian. Because of these experiences, I promised myself that I would never again make a political or theological compromise with racism. Racism is a deadly disease that must be resisted by any means necessary. Never again would I ever expect white racists to do right in relation to the black community. A moral or theological appeal based on a white definition of morality or theology will always serve as a detriment to our attainment of black freedom. The only option we blacks have is to fight in every way possible, so that we can begin to create a definition of freedom based on our own history and culture. We must not expect white people to give us freedom. Freedom is not a gift, but a responsibility, and thus must be taken against the will of those who hold us in bondage.

The writing of *Black Theology and Black Power* that summer was a therapeutic and a liberating experience for me. It is an understatement to say that I did not attempt to write a "balanced" and "objective" view regarding black-white relations in theology, church, and society. I knew whose side I was on and I was not going to allow my training in white "academic scholarship" to camouflage my feelings. With a Ph.D. degree, I had already demonstrated that I knew how to play the academic game. Furthermore, since the academic game in theology and other disciplines had little to do with black people's self-determination, why should I let the ethos of the white seminary or university control the content and the form of my writing?

When it became clear to me that my intellectual consciousness should be defined and controlled by black history and culture and not by standards set in white seminaries and universities, I could feel in the depth of my being a liberation that began to manifest itself in the energy and passion of my writing. Writing for the first time became as natural as talking and preaching. Of course, they were not identical, but writing was no longer an alien experience. It became a joyful experience, a creation of a

perspective on life that I could objectify and analyze in the
ecstasy of my engagement with the black experience.

In addition to being therapeutic and liberating, the writing of
Black Theology and Black Power was also a conversion experience.
It was like experiencing the death of white theology and being
born again into the theology of the black experience. A foretaste
of this rebirth occurred in my writing of "Christianity and Black
Power." But its full manifestation did not happen until the
writing of my first book on black theology. I now realized why it
was so difficult for me to make the connection between the black
experience and theology. As long as theology was exclusively
defined by whites, the connection could never be made because
of their racism. Racists do not define theology in a way that
challenges their racism. To expect white theologians to
voluntarily make theology relevant to black people's struggle for
justice would be like expecting Pharaoh in Egypt to voluntarily
liberate Israelites from slavery. It is the victims and those who
identify with them who must make the connection between their
struggle and the gospel.

Furthermore when the victims of injustice make the
connection between their struggle and the gospel of Jesus, their
oppressors always deny that such a connection exists. As I was
writing my first book on black theology, I knew that the majority
of white theologians and preachers would either ignore it or
denounce it as unchristian and not real theology. But the
anticipation of negative comments from white theologians and
preachers gave me more energy and intensified my passion to
state the case for black theology and against white theology. As
far as I was concerned, the white church and its theology
represented the antichrist and needed to be exposed for what
they were. Indeed I felt "called" by God's Holy Spirit to be an
agent of this exposure.

Of course, I would be less than honest if I failed to
acknowledge the intellectual and religious pride involved in my
newly discovered theological calling. It is always difficult to
distinguish one's own interests and desires from what one
designates as the Holy Spirit. That is why it is important to

develop criteria for distinguishing between human work that comes from God and human activity that is motivated exclusively by human pride. In my case, I felt that despite the presence of my own interest, the reality of God's presence in black people's struggle for justice could hardly be denied by any committed Christian. If this assumption is true, what then is the relationship between my training as a theologian and the black struggle for freedom? For what reason had God allowed a poor black boy from Bearden to become a professional systematic theologian? As I struggled with these questions and the ambiguity involved in my vocation, I could not escape the overwhelming conviction that God's Spirit was calling me to do what I could for the enhancement of justice in the world, especially on behalf of my people. It seemed obvious to me that the best contribution I could make was to uncover the hyprocrisy of the white church and its theology. I had been studying and teaching white theology for more than ten years and had achieved the highest professional degree possible. Not many blacks had my technical training in theology, and no one, not even white theologians, could question my academic credentials. I felt that God must have been preparing me for this vocation, that is, the task of leveling the most devastating black critique possible against the white church and its theology.

As I wrote, I kept thinking about my slave grandparents in Arkansas, Alabama, and Mississippi, and of the silence of white theologians about their struggle to survive the whip and the pistol. I also thought about the auction block and the Underground Railroad, and what both meant for the realities of slavery and black people's struggle to liberate themselves in an extreme situation of oppression. While I had not lived during the time of legal slavery, its impact upon black life was still visibly present in the contemporary economic, social, and political structures of the United States. Lynching is the most dramatic manifestation of the legacy of black slavery. Aside from the memory of the Bearden whites' threat to lynch my father, I also thought about the approximately five thousand documented lynchings in the last half of the nineteenth and the first half of the twentieth centuries,[3] and the support that these demonic acts received from white churches. The more I thought about the oppression of black people and the conspicuous silence of white churches and their theologians, the more determined I became to expose their true character as being demonic and thus unchristian.

I could not avoid thinking of my mother and father, who were still living in Bearden at the time, and their struggle to create a humane and Christian environment for their children. Lucy and Charlie Cone had worked hard and endured much white dehumanization in Bearden so that I could have a sense of worth and self-confidence, thereby enabling me to become a teacher and writer of Christian theology. Therefore I had to say something that would represent the truth of their lives. If I did not do that, then I did not even deserve to be a theologian.

Also dominant on my mind was the fact that none of the major theological interpreters of Europe and North America used the experience of the black poor as a source of doing theology. That was why I could study for years at Garrett-Northwestern and not be required to even read a book on racism or any aspect of the black experience. The one occasion on which I ventured to raise the issue created such chaos that the class had to be dismissed. That kind of experience makes a person bitter and also determined to find ways to render an appropriate judgment upon all who participated in it or identified with it. I knew that most of my former white classmates, professors, and administrators of Garrett would not like what I was writing. But that only pleased me, for I could not forget their attitudes of superiority as white professors and administrators gave all the scholarships and fellowships to white students, as if other blacks and I were too dumb to get one.

It is not possible to endure humiliating experiences like that and not be angry about it. The thing that made me so angry was the knowledge that what had happened to me had happened to many black students at Garrett and also routinely happened at other seminaries at that time. (Unfortunately such things still occur today.) With my own and other black students' humiliating experiences on my mind, everytime I made a cogent theological point, I smiled and said to myself: "This is for Garrett, and what white professors and students did to black students." Whatever else I wanted to achieve, one chief concern was to expose the racism at Garrett in particular and in the white churches and their seminaries in general. When one part of me began to say that maybe I was being a little too hard and perhaps unfair regarding white churches and their theology, there was a stronger side of me that recalled how inhumane white people had been toward black people. The extent of white brutality against my people had been so great that there was no way I could possibly overstate the case for black liberation. White churches and their theology had been so wicked that my little book would not even make a dent in revealing the extent of their evil. My book would be like a fly on a horse's back, annoying perhaps, but with not even a chance of destroying the beast. Why then should I tone down the truth of my claim? Why should I allow a few white exceptions to camouflage the enormity of white people's brutality against black people?

The experience of connecting theology with black history and culture also made me realize more clearly why I had such a difficult time writing in graduate school. How could I write creatively about a history and a people who were so alien to my historical experience? Writing in graduate school was a problem because I never wrote on a subject arising out of black people's history and culture. To be sure, I wrote an M.A. thesis and a Ph.D. dissertation. But as I now look back on that experience, I do not know how I managed to accomplish either task. I certainly would not regard them as important pieces of scholarly work. They were merely necessary chores in my preparation to write black theology.

When a person writes about something that matters to him or her existentially, and in which his or her identity is at stake, then the energy for it comes easily and naturally. The writing is no longer being done for someone else but for oneself as a requirement for survival. One writes because one has to write, and there is no other option. It is like the call to preach or to testify. The spirit of another invades one's being and compels one to tell the truth. That was something of what I felt in writing *Black Theology and Black Power.*

Many people are surprised when I tell them that I did not contact a publisher before I began writing. I never even thought about whether a publisher would be interested in what I was writing. I was writing not for a publisher but for myself, black people, and the divine Spirit, who I believed was compelling me to write. When I finished the book, after writing fourteen to fifteen hours a day for nearly four weeks, I relaxed and held on to it for about two months. Then as a matter of courtesy I sent a copy of what I had written to Eric Lincoln. Within a few days, he called me in Adrian and requested permission to get me a publisher. I was excited that my writing pleased him and that he thought it worthy of publication.

After writing *Black Theology and Black Power,* I knew that the time had come for me to move from the isolated location of Adrian, Michigan. Several invitations came, largely because of the promotion of my work by Eric Lincoln. They included Colgate Rochester Divinity School, San Francisco Theological Seminary, the University of California at Santa Barbara, and Union Theological Seminary in New York. I chose Union over the others because it was located near the largest black community in the United States (Harlem), and because it symbolized the major intellectual forces of white theology. It was the seminary where Reinhold Niebuhr and Paul Tillich had taught, and the place where Daniel Day Williams, Paul Lehmann, John Macquarrie, John Bennett, and Roger Shinn were currently teaching. What other place could I have gone that would have presented the most challenging side of the black and white worlds? I wanted to see if I could make a case for black theology among some of the most respected white theological minds in the country. And being so close to the Harlem community, I thought that the presence of blacks would constantly remind me whence I came and to whom I am ultimately accountable.

The publication of *Black Theology and Black Power* in March

1969 had a much greater impact than I ever anticipated. About one month later, James Forman presented the "Black Manifesto" at Riverside Church, May 4, 1969.[4] The black critique of the white churches and their theology was heard in black and white, secular and religious contexts. During this time, I received an invitation from Metz Rollins, then the executive director of the National Conference of Black Churchmen (NCBC), to become a member of the Theological Commission and also to participate in writing a statement on black theology. In the communication that preceded the meeting, my *Black Theology and Black Power* was recommended as preparation reading.

I was quite pleased about being invited to be a member of the Theological Commission of NCBC and about going to Atlanta to write a black theology statement. The occasion enabled me for the first time to be in dialogue with other black theologians and preachers on the subject of black theology. I was enthusiastically received in Atlanta as if my book represented what the organization was attempting to accomplish. At the time I was working on my second book, *A Black Theology of Liberation*, and thus the word "liberation," though found in *Black Theology and Black Power*, was now the central idea for articulating the gospel of Jesus. I suggested defining black theology as a theology of black liberation. It was accepted without dissent. James Forman's Black Manifesto was also strongly supported.[5]

Later I was invited to make the major presentation for the fall convocation of NCBC in Oakland, California. It was within the ecumenical context of NCBC that my work on black theology received its strongest support. Everyone in the organization encouraged me in my writing, always reminding me of its importance. While white theologians were either silent or criticized me for being too narrow or exclusive, the women and men of NCBC were saying "amen" and "right on." They let me know that I was on the right track, and that I was not alone in the struggle to make sense out of the gospel in the context of our fight for freedom. NCBC was the organizational and political implementation of my theological perspective. It provided the practical context for me to make the connection between the gospel and the black liberation struggle. Without NCBC I would have been removed from the church self-consciously engaged in political struggle, because the black denominations were too conservative and also too busy with their own organizational machinery to embrace black theology.

Black Theology and Black Power also received a wide audience among black nationalist groups, especially the Congress of African People (CAP) which was led by Amiri Baraka (LeRoi Jones). I first met Baraka in Newark and he later invited me to be one of the leaders of the religion workshop at CAP's major meeting in Atlanta in September 1970. Although nationalist groups liked my critique of black and white churches, they did not like my attempt to reread the Bible in the light of black people's struggle for freedom. For them, Christianity was the white man's religion, used to enslave the minds of Africans so that they would not resist slavery and colonization. Therefore no amount of rereading of the white man's Bible could make it acceptable to black nationalists. African people need their own religion, the nationalists argued, and not a reinterpretation of the white man's religion. Our religion must be African in origin, as we are. How can we Africans proclaim that "it's nation time," a time for an assertion of our total liberation, if we do not have a religion derived exclusively from our history and culture?

The intensity and passion with which black nationalists advocated their religious views did not leave any room for debate. I wanted to tell them that Christianity was not European in origin and that the white denominations in North America represented the opposite of Jesus' gospel. But unless I was prepared to embrace the Black Christian Nationalism of Albert Cleage[6], my points would have gotten me nowhere. For intellectual and other reasons, I could not endorse the nationalist perspective of Cleage. What then was I to do?

I decided to take the occasion as an opportunity to learn about black nationalism from the inside. Of the nearly one hundred people in the religion workshop, no one publicly endorsed the traditional black church or the Christianity associated with it.

Christianity was vehemently rejected as white and evil, and black churches were universally condemned for identifying salvation with a white Jesus. While nationalists were not in agreement about *which* black religion ought to be the universal religion for all blacks, they were in agreement in their rejection of the religion of the traditional black churches.

As one of the leaders of the workshop, I spent most of my time overseeing heated debates among nationalists. They were dogmatic not only in their rejection of Christianity, but also in their rejection of one another's version of black religion. Seeing and hearing the disrespect with which nationalists treated one another cured my romanticism about the affirmation of blackness as the only requirement for a successful black liberation struggle. The mere agreement that white people are devils is not enough to attain our freedom. We must agree not only about what we are against but also about what we are for. I was especially troubled by the lack of any genuine dialogue. Everyone simply made speeches either affirming or rejecting some previously expressed view. There was constant shouting and name calling, but at no time did any advocate of a particular view give the impression of listening to the opposition for the purpose of learning from him or her.

Most disturbing to me were the constant insults that nationalists hurled at the black church. It was not that I thought that the black church was above criticism. On the contrary, it needed to be criticized, and I had done just that in *Black Theology and Black Power*. But the problem with the nationalists' criticisms was that they missed the mark because they did not know anything about black churches. Nationalists advanced the same criticisms of black churches found in the white media and in white colleges and universities. If white people were racist regarding their views of the black community as a whole why then did nationalists readily accept their view of black churches as otherworldly and compensatory? Unfortunately, black nationalists did not even know that they were giving a *white* critique of the black churches, and they were too dogmatic to recognize it after being told. When people think that they have the whole truth and nothing but, they cannot hear another viewpoint even when it comes from another who has lived a similar history. Black nationalists were so absolute in their condemnation of the black church that they appeared not to recognize the implied contradiction of holding their meeting at the Interdenominational Theological Center, a black seminary, and Morris Brown College, a black college of the AME Church. When the major leaders of CAP met to discuss their financial difficulties, some persons even suggested asking black churches for money. I hardly knew whether to laugh or cry.

The CAP meeting in Atlanta[7] helped me to rethink my place in black nationalist organizations. How could I be a member of nationalist groups that insultingly rejected the black church and biblical Christianity, both of which had been so important in my early life in Bearden? Rejecting the black church and the Bible would have been like rejecting my mother and father, and I could not do that. I did not do it on the basis of the erroneous arguments of white theologians at Garrett, and I was not prepared to do it on the basis of similar arguments of black nationalists in Atlanta. Although I recognized some truth in the nationalists' arguments, it was clear to me that, like white theologians, they did not really know the black church they were critcizing. Their criticisms were too simple and thus did not reflect the complexity of the past and contemporary black church. Alongside the conservative, otherworldly black church is also the radical, this-worldly black church. The latter was often latent and the former was more visible. But we must ask why it was latent and not recognizable to all. The nationalists' lack of interest in a serious analysis of that question put me on the fringe of their movement.

A similar problem occurred with other black revolutionary groups, especially the ones influenced by Karl Marx. All were equally dogmatic in their rejection of the black church as being too politically conservative and religiously otherworldly. I will never forget the speech that David Hilliard of the Black Panthers gave to black Christians (mainly preachers) at the NCBC Convocation in Oakland. I have never heard anyone so rude and insulting as he was on that occasion. Aside from his unrepeatable expletives, Hilliard told black preachers that unless they were prepared to put down the Bible and pick up the gun to shoot white policemen, then he and other Panthers would shoot them as they shoot policemen. After hearing Hilliard and others like him, I realized the extent to which white oppression had twisted the minds of our revolutionary leaders. How could they lead when they could not think straight or clearly? How could they claim to love the black community when they could not even take the time to understand the role of the church in our mental and physical struggle, I came to the conclusion that I could not participate in a revolution that did not include my mother! And she believed in Jesus and was firmly committed to the black church. That meant that my primary involvement had to be in the black church and only secondarily in black nationalist and Marxist organizations. With this conviction clear in my mind, NCBC became the main context for me to work out the meaning of black theology.

During the early 1970s, white and black theologians began to respond to my perspective on black theology. Most whites said that I was too exclusive, and many blacks said that I was not exclusive enough. In listening to their critiques for the purpose of a response, the contextual character of theological language became increasingly clear to me.

Although most white theologians gave the predictable responses to my perspective, some showed a sophisticated understanding of it and also a commitment to relating the gospel to the struggles of the oppressed. Among them were William Hordern, Fred Herzog, and Paul Lehmann.

When I wrote my first essay entitled "Christianity and Black Power," I sent a copy to William Hordern, who had left Garrett to become the president of a Lutheran seminary in Canada. He responded to my essay with strong words of encouragement. My writings on black theology initiated dialogue through correspondence in which he provided continued encouragement and a challenging critique of my theological perspective. For me to be able to correspond with my former teacher created an enormous intellectual excitement and self-confidence. This correspondence reminded me of the dialogue we had in his classes at Garrett, during which time Hordern, in contrast to many other white professors, always made me believe that I could think and say something worthwhile. His vigorous critique against certain weaknesses in my argument was always intended to strengthen the foundation of my perspective on black theology. Not once did he play the academic tricks so prevalent among scholars. He always made it clear that my critique of white theology and affirmation of a black theology were essentially correct. His effort was directed toward deepening my argument by insisting that I should take into account some things that appeared to have been overlooked. I have always enjoyed our dialogues, some of which were recorded for national television and also published in *Christian Century*.[8]

While Hordern's response to black theology was in the form of letters to me, Fred Herzog's comments were directed mainly to the white theological and church public. No white theologian did more than Herzog in making the white church and its theology take note of the justice of black theology's critique. At a time when it was unpopular to support black theology's critical appraisal of white theology, Herzog accepted the critique as the starting point of his theological perspective and refused to let the white theological establishment escape the indictment. His *Liberation Theology*[9] is a major response to black theology, and it did not win him many friends in the white theological and church communities.

Paul Lehmann's response to black theology is also found in his published writings.[10] But I will never forget our dialogues at Union Seminary. During my first year at Union, we had our first of several public debates about black theology in the presence of the Union faculty. Lehmann took black theology very seriously, but he did not endorse it without raising critical questions, especially in relation to violence, reconciliation, and the problem of ideology. My identification of the black revolution with divine revelation troubled him, as it would anyone who took seriously the theological tradition of Calvin, Barth, and Bonhoeffer. My theological tradition was quite different, since it included Nat Turner, Henry M. Turner, and Malcolm X. But since Lehmann and I had an equal commitment to and respect for the scripture as the primary source for doing theology, we always found ourselves in basic theological agreement. He kept pressing me on the question of violence and its reconciliation with the gospel. And I always wanted to know *why* that question was so important to him in speaking about the black struggle for freedom, and *for whom* was he asking it. In black theological contexts, the violence of blacks seems to be the chief question for whites, but in white theological contexts, the issue is seldom raised by whites to themselves. Of course, I knew that Lehmann was not a typical white theologian, and he had more on his mind than the obvious. That was why I learned so much from him, and why even today his theology is a challenge to read.

In addition to Hordern, Herzog, and Lehmann, there were other white theologians in North America and Europe who responded to black theology. The most challenging responses have been in the contexts of the World Council of Churches, the World Methodist Council, and many universities, seminaries, and colleges in Europe and North America. The issues inevitably focused on the question of violence, love, and ideology. Because I did not condemn violence and identify love with nonviolence, white theologians questioned whether I had reduced theology to the politics of black liberation. Because I did not bother to relieve them of their fears, I often stated black theology's case so as to confirm them. My object was to identify the gospel with the historical struggles of the victims and not with the concerns of white theologians.[11]

Much more important than the responses of white theologians were the responses of black theologians. I had naïvely assumed that the initial enthusiastic responses of black theologians to the publication of my *Black Theology and Black Power* meant that they agreed with my perspective on black theology. But that was not always the case. The first radical disagreement came from Charles Long and Carleton Lee. Long was then teaching at the University of Chicago, and Lee at Western Michigan University. I was shocked that the criticism was so severe and also voiced the concerns of other black scholars. Gayraud S. Wilmore and my brother Cecil joined the dialogue and sided with Long and Lee against me. I was stunned for some time and did not know what response to make.

The issue focused on the question of whether I was really doing black theology or white theology that was merely painted black. Charles Long even questioned whether a black theology was possible since theology itself is European and thus imperialistic by its very nature. He contended that history of religion, a discipline more value-free in its aproach, was the best tool for examining black religion. While Wilmore's and Cecil Cone's critiques were similar, they did not question the legitimacy of black theology. Rather they contended that black theology must not be identified primarily, if at all, with biblical Christianity, but should be identified with the history and culture of black people stretching back to African religions. Therefore the chief sources of black theology should not be the Bible, Jesus Christ, or any other theological norm that did not come from black people's African origins.

Lee, Long, Wilmore, and Cecil Cone agreed that my theological perspective was too dependent on white theology. They claimed that both *Black Theology and Black Power* and *A Black Theology of Liberation* used conceptual categories that came from Europe and not Africa. This meant that I had not been fully liberated from the rational structure of Western thought forms. If theology is black, they asked, must not the sources used for its articulation also be black? Where are the black sources in James Cone? To be sure, he refers to a few black preachers of the nineteenth century, but they are not essential to the content of his theological message or the form that the argument takes. They are simply used as tokens in a theological system derived from white theology.

I listened to this critique for nearly two years and concluded that they were partly correct, at least enough to make me think more deeply about the nature of black theology. I was embarrassed by this critique, because no one had been more critical of white theology than I. To find out from my black colleagues that I was still held captive by the same system that I was criticizing was a bitter pill to swallow. What then was I to do? Deny the obvious or give up in despair? I decided to do neither. I reminded myself that theology is human discourse, and it is to be expected to have certain weaknesses, because no one can know the whole truth. The issue is whether I had identified an aspect of the truth of the gospel, despite shortcomings, and whether I had an openness to learn from others. Since I was absolutely sure that I was right about liberation being the central motif of the gospel and one of the most creative elements of black religion, what I needed to do was to rethink the content and shape of black theology in that light. The writing of *The Spirituals and the Blues* (1972) represented my first effort to take seriously the critique of black theologians. *God of the Oppressed* (1975) is a continuation of that dialogue. I realize that I have not answered my critics to their satisfaction and probably never will. But they do know that I tried to hear and to learn from them. My response to them about their own weaknesses is found in my essay "An Interpretation of the Debate Among Black Theologians."[12] I do not have anything to add to that response except to observe that my critics on black religion have not been able to write the kind of black theological studies that they accused me of not writing.

By contrast one cannot accuse J. Deotis Roberts of not writing a theological text based on his critique of my theological program. Although sharing some sympathies with my black religion critics, his major concern was to reject my apparent exclusive focus on political liberation. In his first book, *Liberation and Reconciliation: A Black Theology*,[13] he challenged me to deal with reconciliation and not only liberation. The gospel has primarily to do with love and the reconciliation of blacks and whites. For me to focus exclusively on political liberation, to an apparent exclusion of a community that includes blacks and whites together, seemed to Roberts like denying the essence of the gospel.

I was surprised by Roberts' critique, because it sounded like a white criticism. I learned later that Roberts was also representing the concerns of many preachers in black churches. Also Major Jones' *Black Awareness: A Theology of Hope*[14] seemed to support Roberts' concern. My response has been given in *God of the Oppressed* and in my essay "An Interpretation of the Debate Among Black Theologians." In my reply, I said that they were wrong, as were white theologians. To introduce reconciliation and love, as Roberts and others had done, was to minimize the alienation that white racism had created. In view of the black struggle for freedom in North America for nearly four hundred years and in view of the black civil rights and Black Power struggles of the 1950s and 60s, how could Roberts make reconciliation a central category of black theology? That term was too misleading and suggested the wrong emphasis. The riots had occurred with many blacks left dead in the streets. Richard Nixon was President, and black radicals were being shot on sight. How could anyone make reconciliation a central black theological category in such a time as that? My response to Roberts has been more severe because he seemed to have ignored the obvious by saying what whites wanted to hear.

When William Jones wrote *Is God a White Racist?*[15] he introduced the problem of theodicy in black theology in a manner that no black theologian could ignore. If God is liberating black people from oppression, where is the empirical evidence to warrant that claim? Where is the exaltation-liberation event in black history that would make black theology's reference to God as the liberator credible?

Jones' critique of black theology forced me to think more deeply about the meaning of theological language when connected with black people's struggle for freedom. (My response to him is found in the same places as are my responses to other black theologians.) Jones' critique was penetrating and cogent and could not be dismissed easily. I had to wrestle with him. I concluded that there was no answer to the problem of suffering that would satisfy people who stand outside of the black community of faith. And even for persons of faith, the problem is not solved, because there is no answer that faith can give for suffering that removes its contradiction. Faith in Christ therefore does not explain evil; it empowers us to fight against evil. Faith prevents compromise and despair in the encounter with evil. But faith does not make evil acceptable or account for its existence. Evil remains inexplicable, not in spite of faith but because of it. In the struggle against evil, we encounter the "crucified God" (Jürgen Moltmann's phrase) in the suffering of the victims of history. This encounter of the suffering God discloses that humanity's ultimate future is not reducible to the scientific and rational categories of history. This is an eschatological realm that transcends this world.

When we make the move toward the eschatological as the lens through which we analyze reality, we are using a language that has been created and nurtured in the history and struggles of the oppressed. My earlier writings were critical of the eschatology found in black religion, because my dependency on white theology and politics blinded me to the revolutionary force inherent in the black concept of heaven. The critiques of Charles Long, Gay Wilmore, and Cecil Cone forced me to take a closer look at black eschatology. In my study of the spirituals, gospels, sermons, and prayers of black people, the intricacies of eschatology became clear to me. I also reflected on its use in Bearden, Arkansas. This new way of analyzing black eschatology helped me to answer Jones' critique. If I accepted the humanistic premise of Jones, the cogency of his logic is irrefutable. But if there is a realm of reality that is eschatological, then evil and suffering do not have the last word. For what is, is also coming to be. This was precisely the message of the black spirituals and of black religion generally. Because black slaves believed that what is was coming to be, they refused to let their humanity be defined by the historical limitations of slavery. Black eschatology became a source of empowerment for slaves, enabling them to act as if

> Nobody knows who I am,
> Till the judgment morning.

3

Black Theology and the Black Church

The severity of my criticisms of the black church and my initial endorsement of the politics of Black Power often camouflaged the fact that I was born in a Christian home and nurtured to adulthood in the black church. After joining Macedonia AME Church in Bearden at the age of ten, I preached my first sermon at sixteen in my brother's church, Spring Hill AME, near Little Rock, on December 12, 1954. Between the ages of seventeen and twenty, as a student at Shorter and Philander Smith colleges, I pastored San Hill, Spring Hill, and Allen Chapel AME churches. When I left Little Rock for divinity school in Evanston, I did intend to return to Arkansas as pastor of an AME church. While in the Chicago-Evanston area, I preached in many AME churches and was soon appointed an assistant pastor at Woodlawn AME Church on Chicago's South Side.

My plans for returning to Arkansas as an AME pastor were changed during my last years on the bachelor of divinity degree when the AME bishop in Arkansas informed me that no churches were available and none were expected to come open in the near future. I was shocked and very disappointed. However, I had been an AME preacher long enough to read between the lines. The issue involved not merely the availability of churches but also internal church politics designed to prevent the "Cone boys" (as Cecil and I were called) from returning home. My brother was fortunate to be appointed to Sanders Memorial AME church in Detroit, Michigan. But when I inquired among several AME bishops about the possibility of an appointment, I was informed that nothing was available. With two bachelors degrees (one in religion and philosophy and the other in theology) and no church, I was left with no alternative but to try to stay in graduate school for the M.A. and Ph.D. degrees at Garrett-Northwestern in order to prepare myself for the teaching ministry.

I was not bitter because I understood the nature of AME Church politics. I remained deeply involved in my denomination, attending its major meetings, and offering to serve in whatever capacity was appropriate and nonpolitical in the church. I actually felt relieved, because now I was completely certain that my vocation was for the teaching ministry. This meant that I could be involved in the work of my denomination without having to compromise my integrity and commitment in order to receive an appointment commensurate with my experience and ability.

When I was near the completion of my doctoral work, I inquired again among bishops, college and seminary presidents, and other church leaders about a teaching position in one of our AME schools, because I wanted to remain closely identified with my denomination. While I did not expect miracles, neither did I anticipate what appeared to me as a complete indifference to my plight. Again I was told that nothing was available. At this point, I was getting a little disturbed. If my church had no available teaching post, something hard to believe since I was one of a very few AMEs with a Ph.D. degree, its major leaders could at least show some concern about my future. Fortunately, I was able to acquire a teaching position at Philander Smith, a Methodist College. Even after this appointment, I still had hopes of eventually acquiring a teaching job in an AME college. This hope was almost realized at Morris Brown College in Atlanta, but President Frank Cunningham died the night before my arrival there to sign the contract. The AME bishop who chaired the board of directors, the sole authority at the time, did not honor the late president's verbal commitment.

After being denied an opportunity to serve the AME church as a pastor and teacher, I began to think of the black church in more theological and ecumenical terms. That meant that a particular denomination was much less important than was the central theme of black liberation that ought to define the identity of all black churches. The issue then was not whether a denomination was AME, AME Zion, Baptist, Methodist, Roman Catholic, Pentecostal, or a host of other names black churches used to describe their Christian identity. Rather, the issue was whether a denomination was a community of believers called into being by God in order to participate in the divine work to set the captives free. If a black denomination did not meet the criterion of liberation, as defined by both the Bible and black history, then it was no different from white churches and thus must be exposed for its apostasy. Like white churches, black denominations that ignored the liberation of the poor as their central message were not the people of God but rather the agents of the anti-Christ. Any denomination, white or black, that defined its essential nature in terms of the selfish aspirations of its leaders or in terms of any other human factor could not be the church of the crucified and risen Lord.

During the 1960s and afterward, it seemed to me that the AME Church and many other black denominations did not regard the liberation of the poor as the central theme of the gospel. Most black denominations preached a "spiritual" gospel that ignored the political plight of the black poor. By failing to connect the gospel with the bodily liberation of the poor, black churches forgot about their unique historical and theological identity and began to preach a gospel no different from that of white churches. That was why black churches did not bother to encourage their historical and contemporary affirmation of faith. For them, unfortunately, black faith was the same as white faith, and thus black churches continued to use the theologies and creeds of the white churches from which they had separated.

Of course, I realized that there was a host of black pastors and preachers who transcended the limitation of their denominations. The civil rights movement of the 1950s and 60s would have been impossible apart from the support of black churches, especially preachers. In fact, the leadership of the movement was overwhelmingly black ministers. The Southern Christian Leadership Conference, which Martin King headed, was made up almost entirely of ministers. The prominence of the role of the black churches in the Freedom movement explains why so many black churches were bombed in the south. The bombing of the Sixteenth Street Baptist Church in Birmingham, Alabama, in which four black girls were killed (1963), is the best known incident. The Progressive Baptist Convention was organized in 1962 partly because of radical black ministers' rejection of the conservative leadership of J. H. Jackson of the National Baptist Convention. Whatever else that we say about the black church, the black struggle for freedom, symbolized by the leadership of Martin King in the civil rights movement, was initiated and run by black preachers. These preachers may not have been Marxists, nationalists, or revolutionary enough for Black Power advocates and black university students and professors; but they risked their lives for black freedom, which is more than can be said of many of their critics.

But when all the credit has been given black preachers and their churches, we must be careful not to romanticize the role of the black church in the civil rights movement. Indeed the extent of the progressive and radical black preachers' commitment can be more clearly appreciated and evaluated when one realizes that they represented a critical minority in black churches. They acted as individuals and upon their own initiative and not as agents of the denominations of which they were members. No black church denomination *as an institution* defined its life and work primarily in terms of the empowerment of the poor in their fight for justice.

To be sure, it is important to point out that, unlike many white denominations, no black denomination, to my knowledge, has ever dismissed a minister for his or her involvement in the fight for justice. While white churches dismissed many ministers for taking a stand for justice, black churches pointed to black ministers' involvement in civil rights as evidence of their own participation in the struggle for justice. This was and still remains an important distinction between black and white churches. Black churches have always allowed themselves to be used as an umbrella under which black ministers could be involved in radical politics with impunity. But white ministers have not been provided such protection. In the white church, the gospel has been so closely identified with American values that any radical challenge of the society usually involves the risk of dismissal from the denomination.

This significant difference between the two churches, however, does not mean that the black church is Christian and the white church is not. To be Christian, the church must be more than an umbrella under which to strive for freedom. It must be an instrument of freedom's realization in the world. During the 1960s, I was disappointed with the AME Church and other black denominations not because of how my church treated me personally, but because of their apparent contentment with being an umbrella of freedom rather than an instrument of its realization. Black churches permitted their preachers and members to be involved in the political struggle for justice, but never made it a requirement for their Christian identity. The Christian identity of black churches was defined as transcending political struggle and not as being derived from it. In this sense, black churches' Christian identity was very similar to the Christian identity of white churches. This meant that it was possible to be a Christian without a concrete historical validation of it through political engagement.

When one's Christian identity is ahistorical and thus exclusively spiritual or otherworldly, then it is possible, perhaps necessary, to separate the gospel from the fight for political justice. White churches make the separation between faith and justice only when their own sociopolitical interests are not at stake, but never when they are. (Note especially the recent switch from the separation of religion and politics to their identity by Jerry Falwell and the Moral Majority.) But black churches make the separation between religion and politics even when black people's political future is in jeopardy. The reason for this theological blindness is that many black churches have internalized the religious values of whites even though they worship separately.

Unfortunately, black churches have allowed the historical and theological identity of black faith to be forgotten partly because of their promotion of the art of preaching to the exclusion of doing theology. Few black Christians know or even care to know about the theological significance of Richard Allen's departure from St. George's Methodist Church or Bishop Henry M. Turner's proclamtion that "God is a Negro."[1] It is like white Protestants in Europe not knowing the religious meaning of the Reformation or the theological significance of Luther's emphasis on "justification by faith." What is even more revealing is that black Baptists are more likely to know about Roger Williams than about Andrew Bryan, and AMEs have probably heard more about John Wesley than about Richard Allen. It is a sad commentary on the history of the black church that its ministers and members know so little about the *theological* reasons for their existence.

Theology is the critical side of faith, and without it faith loses its distinctive identity. Preaching is the proclamation of the faith, and without it faith cannot be genuinely celebrated. Preaching and theology are indispensable for the life and work of the church. How can the gospel be heard apart from the one who preaches the Word? But how do we know that the preached word is bearing witness to the Word made flesh if there is no critical evaluation of the preacher's proclamation? Theology provides a critical test for the church so as to determine whether its life and work are consistent with the person and work of Jesus Christ. If a church has no theologians, then it cannot be genuinely self-critical and thereby seek to overcome its shortcomings and weaknesses. Black churches have not encouraged the development of theology alongside their strong emphasis on preaching. The consequence of this failure is the absence of self-criticism and thus a loss of the churches' distinct religious identity.

When a church loses its identity, it no longer knows its proper mission and consequently loses itself in organizational routine. That was precisely what I observed in the AME Church and other black denominations. During the 1960s and afterward, most of the time and energy of black churches was devoted to electing bishops and other officers, calling and appointing preachers, and building and buying church edifices. The essence of the church appeared to be limited to that of running the organization as defined by internal church politics. There was almost no time set aside or context created for asking the critical questions: What is the Church? Has the AME Church remained faithful to its essence as defined by Jesus Christ? How can the Church be what it ought to be if it does not critically ask about its own identity?

After many years of being a minister in the AME Church, I concluded that there was no way that I could be a true theologian of my church and also be employed by it. The power and authority of the bishops was nearly absolute and often arbitrary. I could not place my personhood at the disposal of AME bishops. I had observed the public humiliation of many ministers when they attempted to make a bishop accountable to human decency and respect. When I first saw it in Arkansas, I knew then that I would never be able to accept such treatment from anyone. Perhaps the internalization of my father's refusal to submit to white racists was so great that I not only rebelled against the unjust authority of whites but also refused to accept the inhumane authority of AME bishops. I could not develop the appropriate deference needed to be accepted by most whites or to be a successful AME preacher. Even if I had been fortunate enough to find a teaching position in an AME college or seminary, it became increasingly clear that I would not have escaped the authority of the bishop and thus I would not have been free to criticize the church on the basis of the gospel.

The major test used to determine one's commitment to the AME Church was one's willingness to accept without question the authority and power of the bishop in all church matters. A true AME minister was expected to endure much personal suffering and also to be obedient to superiors, with appropriate deference and the acknowledgment that the superiors knew more about what was best for the church than any newcomer or outsider. I did not mind the personal suffering as long as the suffering was necessary for the gospel, shared by all, and not caused by the arbitrary whim of the AME bishop. Though not always, too often the nature and extent of a minister's suffering was exclusively determined by the religious and political disposition of a particular AME bishop. To be sure, not all AME bishops were inhumane and arbitrary in the exercise of their episcopal power. But the problem of the lack of accountability of episcopal power was pervasive enough for me to conclude that there was no way that I could be a critical theologian and also be controlled by AME bishops.

When I raised these problems with prominent AME preachers who themselves were aspiring for the episcopacy (an aspiration that almost all AME ministers have), they often minimized them by appealing to the blackness of their church identity: The *African* Methodist Episcopal Church. With a black theologian of my perspective, they knew that an appeal to our cultural and historical roots would carry much weight in our discussion. In order to defend the AME Church against my contemporary critique, they would base their reply almost exclusively upon the past history of the church. They would retell the story of Richard Allen, who walked out of St. George's Methodist Church in 1787 in Philadelphia, because he refused to accept segregated worship as consistent with his Christian identity. Included in the AME story was its founding in 1816; the association of Morris Brown (later to become the church's second bishop) with the Denmark Vesey's 1822 insurrection; Bishop Daniel Payne's educational leadership; and Bishop Henry M. Turner's black nationalism and missionary work in Africa. But what was most revealing about the proclamation of this historical "roll call" was that many persons who spoke the loudest about it and who gave the most passionate "Amen!" to it knew very little about the theological and historical significance of the names that were called. Furthermore, it would have been virtually impossible to get the AME denomination to set aside the necessary financial resources for serious theological and historical research on the persons to whom they appealed for credibility. As a consequence, the average AME preacher, not to mention the layperson, hardly knew anything about the historical origin and theological significance of their church. That was why I could not take seriously prominent AME preachers' public identification with blackness through slogan-eering and sermonic rhetoric.

When I suggested that the glorification of the past could not in any way serve as an excuse for the current moral corruption of the AME Church, many ministers asked me whether I would rather be in a white church under white bishops and superiors. That was a legitimate question that deserved and received a serious response. I said that being a minister in a white church was analogous to being a teacher in a white college, university, and seminary. And being a minister in a black church was like teaching in a black school. I have served in both contexts. In the white context, whether school or church, one knew or ought to have known that the organization was not defined primarily for the liberation of the black poor. When whites therefore resisted black liberation, that was only what they had been doing for more than four hundred years. No black person should be a minister in a white denomination on the assumption that it is devoted to the gospel as defined by black history. Membership in white organizatons, whether school or church, should be because of the belief that, despite many shortcomings, the white organization provides a meaningful context in which to work on behalf of the black struggle for freedom. It was this perspective that motivated me to accept a teaching post at Adrian College and later Union Theological Seminary.

Shortly after I accepted a teaching post at Union, John Bennett, then president, called me into his office to inquire about my reference to the white church as the anti-Christ. "Jim, you do not mean that literally, do you?" he asked. I responded carefully and with appropriate respect: "John, I do not mean to be rude to you or to anybody; I only wish to speak the truth. As I see it, the white church is the opposite of the true meaning of Jesus Christ. I mean it literally." "But why did you choose to teach at Union if you mean it literally?" he asked. "John, my father cut billets and logs for a living, and I work at Union," I said. "And as long as I have to support my family, I might as well do it here. Living in a racist society, every black person has to assume that his job may not meet all the requirements for which he or she may have been called."

It is appropriate here to say a word about Union since my coming in 1969. My work as a teacher has become increasingly more consistent with my calling. Far more than I anticipated, Union has made a genuine effort to define theological education in such a manner that it explicitly includes persons who are concerned for the liberation of the poor. I would be the first to admit that Union has not gone as far in this direction as it should. But when Union is compared with other white seminaries like it, no school, to my knowledge, has ever come close to making the commitment that Union has. It is the only white seminary that I know of that seeks to include Third World people's culture, history, and theology at the center of the educational process along with the traditional European models. That was why I moved from being indifferent about Union to being committed to an implementation of its public expressions of being a seminary for all and not only for whites.

My statement about Union does not mean that I regard it as being an example of my definition of the gospel. It represents some important aspects of my understanding of the gospel but not enough to be regarded as an embodiment of it. But it is enough for me to give my intellectual commitment to it. In this regard, I think it is important to point out that I do not expect Union to ever represent my definition of the gospel perfectly. Nor do I wish Union to do it. Union is a pluralistic community with many different constituencies, only one of which is black. The pluralistic nature of Union's community is what makes it an exciting place in which to teach. I do not wish it to become a black seminary, and I will fight to keep it from becoming an exclusively white one. Union needs to be a community of Asians, Africans, Latin Americans, black Americans, Hispanic Americans, white Americans, women of all races and cultures, and a host of other kinds of people. Union needs to be a seminary that symbolizes the universal meaning of the gospel, both in the people who study and teach there as well as in the content of what is studied.

Although Union has not reached that goal, that is the dream of many who teach and study there. It appears sometime that other people at Union have other things in mind, even when they say otherwise. That means that Union is always in danger of retreating from its commitment. If that should ever happen, I will have to do my part in fighting against it. But at this writing, Union, despite its white origins and dominance, is a meaningful and exciting place in which to do theology. I know that many people at Union do not agree with my theological perspective, and that is one thing that makes it exciting. Other perspectives on the gospel challenge me to think more deeply about the meaning of the gospel. They help me to locate weaknesses in my theological perspectives which, apart from their challenge, I would probably overlook. Indeed, I firmly believe that one's critic in theology is often one's best friend.

When I reflect on the 1960s, the time when I taught at Philander Smith and was also a minister in the AME Church, I expected my vocation as a teaching minister to be more clearly realized than it could ever be in a white context. In a black context, the very existence of a church or school was designed primarily for the empowerment of black people. Therefore when Philander Smith and the AME Church began to contradict their public commitment to black people's freedom, I could not remain silent about it. How could any committed person remain silent in the context where black leaders used the church and other institutions for the achievement of their own personal ambitions? It was not that I thought or have ever thought that the white church or school was a more creative context to work in than a black one. The issue was one of expectation. As black students should expect more of a black professor than a white one, similarly I expected more of our black schools and churches than of white ones. Therefore when black leaders of our churches and schools sought to escape accountability by pointing to white institutions as being worse, I responded, "True. So what?"

My disappointment with the AME Church during the 1960s led me to conclude that blackness alone was not enough. The church's blackness must be determined not exclusively by skin color, but rather by its obedience to God's call to be in concrete solidarity with the poor who are struggling for freedom. In retrospect, the most serious problem was the failure of the AME Church to provide a context in which the theological identity of the church could be evaluated.

Because I was excluded from participating as a theologian in the AME Church, and because I concluded that membership in a particular historical black denomination was less important than a contemporary political commitment to the liberation of black people, I decided to leave the AME Church and to become a United Methodist. As I have already suggested in my distinction between the black and white churches, the decision to become a United Methodist did not mean that I thought it was more Christian than the AME Church. That possibility never occurred to me. My reasons for becoming a United Methodist related to my teaching in one of its colleges, the warm reception of the black United Methodists to my ministry, and the emergence of the Black Methodists for Church Renewal, about which more will be said.

The critique that I made of the black church must also be made of black theologians, like me, who often escape the practical problems of life with recourse to their theories. Black

76

theologians who do theology apart from the life of the church in the world are just as guilty of apostasy as the black church that loses itself in organizational routine. Black theology must arise out of the struggle of black life. Attending professional societies (white or black), reading and writing books, and teaching in seminaries are not enough. Indeed they must be secondary to our active participation in the praxis of the liberation struggle. Without a concrete obedience that validates our theology, what we say in lectures and books is just as hypocritical and morally suspect as the black church that we criticize. When black theologians are compared with black preachers, it seems clear that neither one has much to talk about that is an advancement over the other. Too many black professors in university and seminary contexts are content with their professional status, with its salary and tenure. Not enough black professors take the risk to fight for a justice that extends beyond their own job security. In this sense, they are like bishops and other black preachers who use the church for their own personal aggrandizement.

Despite appearances to the contrary, I think that black professors are still too captivated by the structures of white thought and therefore cannot think creatively. What we think and how we organize our ideas are too much determined by our training at Union, Harvard, Yale, and other white schools that imitate them. The academic structure of white seminary and university curriculums require that black students reject their heritage or at least regard it as intellectually marginal. When black students study the Bible and church history, almost nothing is said about black people's heritage that would suggest that they have anything to contribute intellectually in those areas. The same is often true for the areas of systematic theology and philosophy of religion, even though black theology emerged as a challenge to that assumption. How is it possible for a black student to get a Ph.D. in theology, biblical studies, or church history and not think that the black church and community have nothing to contribute to those disciplines? Is not an identity crisis inevitable by the very act of becoming a black professor?

As I reflect over my fourteen years of writing and teaching black theology, I am embarrassed by the extent of my captivation by white concepts. And I realize that I am still partly enslaved by them. The struggle to overcome this enslavement has been a constant struggle in my intellectual development. That is why I will always be indebted to my black colleagues for assisting me in this endeavor. Black theologians must continually seek to liberate ourselves from an inordinate dependence upon white theology and philosophy without falling into the trap of promoting undisciplined black rhetoric and sloganeering. We must develop rigorous self-criticism and not tolerate poor academic scholarship.

Black theology's self-criticism should arise from its engagement with the black church and community. As I have criticized the black church, so the church must judge its theologians. Black theology's chief task is not to be an *academic* discipline, as white theology has largely become. Black theology must be a *church* discipline, true to itself only when validated in the context of people struggling for the freedom of the oppressed. Its chief task is to help the church to be faithful to the task of preaching and living the liberating gospel of Jesus Christ in the world today.

Because I realize that doing theology is the responsibility of many persons working as a team, I have devoted much of my time at Union Theological Seminary toward the academic preparation of persons who will share in this responsibility. In my teaching of theology, the emphasis has been on strict academic preparation combined with active participation in the black church and community on behalf of the liberation of the poor. There can be no creative black theology without a disciplined mind, without a solid knowledge of black, third-world, and white theological traditions as they are related to sociology, psychology, philosophy, and history. But how this knowledge is to be used should be decided by our love for the poor. Love demands that we participate in their liberation struggle, fighting against the forces of oppression. Creative black theology can emerge only out of the struggle for black liberation and *not before* or *apart from* that struggle. Black theology must never be allowed to degenerate into mere university or seminary theology. It is and must remain a theology of and for black people arising out of the active political struggle to create a just society in order to bear witness to the coming of God's kingdom.

Since the church and its theologians should be in dialogue, my problem in the late 1960s was to locate "the church" for my own participation. Therefore I was pleased with the emergence of Black Methodists for Church Renewal. Attending their first meeting in Cincinnati in February 1968, I was impressed by what I heard and saw. Black Methodists, at least those who attended the meeting, appeared to be concerned about the gospel's relation to the black liberation struggle and not about internal church politics. In Cincinnati, I saw and met black ministers and laypersons in dialogue with secular Black Power advocates, such as Stokely Carmichael, and black scholars, including C. Eric Lincoln. Since I wanted to be a black theologian who would be in dialogue with both the church and world on behalf of black liberation, I felt at home in the context of black United Methodists generally and BMCR in particular. The latter appeared to be an organizational implementation of my theological understanding of the church.[2]

BMCR represented one of the creative examples of what the black church was called to be and to do in the 1960s. It was a black caucus in the white United Methodist Church. As was true of many black caucuses in white churches, BMCR exposed the racism of whites by relating the Christian faith and the struggle for justice in the black community. It was the initiative of black caucuses in white churches, along with radical black preachers in black churches that created NCBC and later black theology. My entrance into NCBC was preceded by my involvement in BMCR. All black caucuses in white denominations seemed to be enthusiastic in their support of an emerging black consciousness, politically expressed in Black Power and theologically expressed in black theology. Although black caucuses and NCBC respected the work of Martin Luther King, Jr., and the black preachers who supported him in the SCLC, yet we could not remain silent as whites appeared to suggest that their involvement in the Southern civil rights movement gave them the badge of black approval without changing the structures of the church and society in the North. Black Power was the political challenge to the nonviolence of King, because the latter appeared to be more concerned about accommodating white Christianity and liberalism than about the liberation of poor blacks. Black theology was the theological arm of Black Power, seeking to relate the black struggle for freedom to the biblical claim regarding the justice of God.

NCBC was created by an ecumenical group of black churchmen in response to Black Power. It was purposely designed to transcend denominational ties so as to make an unqualified identification with the black liberation struggle. Almost all black denominations were represented, including black Catholics. When I became involved in early 1969, NCBC provided a challenging context for the development of my ideas about black theology. NCBC and BMCR together were two among many places where theological reflection and political action were combined in the struggle for black liberation.

When I wrote *Black Theology and Black Power* (1969) and *A Black Theology of Liberation* (1970), I was not an AME and therefore was not deeply involved in an independent black church denomination. My church involvement was almost exclusively limited to BMCR, NCBC, and other black caucuses that were seeking to address the problem of racism in both church and society. In my encounters with most black denominations of that period, I thought that they were too conservative and thus not interested in relating the gospel to the politics of black liberation. My severe criticism of the black church in *Black Theology and Black Power* arose out of my conviction that it had failed to remain faithful to its heritage of freedom. I was less critical in my second book, *A Black Theology of*

Liberation, not because my views changed but because I felt that whites would use my critique in ways I did not approve.

When my black colleagues criticized me for failing to pay adequate attention to black religion, part of the problem related to my alienation from conservative black churches. That was also why I spoke about the "Underground Church" in my first book. I was searching for an empirical embodiment of what I experienced in the depth of my being and attempted to write in articles and books. The absence of an institutional embodiment made me wonder whether there was a referent to my ideas. If there is no recognizable referent to one's ideas, how does he/she know that what is being articulated is not a figment of his/her theological imagination? NCBC, BMCR, and other black caucuses were at least partial representations of my theological definition of the church.

Although I left the AME denomination, I did not separate myself from the spirit and the truth of the black church. What I had experienced at Macedonia and read about in black church history dominated my theological consciousness. As strange as it may appear to both blacks and whites, the appeal of Karl Barth's theology to my mind and heart was directly related to the control which black religion exerted over my theological consciousness. Three focuses of Barth's theology made his conceptual structure useful in analyzing the black religious experience. They were his emphases upon the threefold form of the Word of God: The Word of God as preached, the written Word of God, and the Revealed Word of God.[5] In Barth's theology, Jesus Christ is the Revealed Word of God. He is the one without whom we cannot speak of God. The Bible is the written form of the Word of God. It is the witness to the Word made flesh. Preaching is the Word of God proclaimed. Each of these manifestations of the Word is interrelated, with Jesus Christ being the foundation of their unity.

When one relates Barth's theology to the black church experience, there are many similarities. Like Barth's theology, Jesus Christ occupies the center of the gospel message in the black church. In sermon, song, prayer, and testimony, Jesus is the one to whom the people turn in times of trouble and distress, because they believe that he can heal their wounded hearts and broken spirits. He is the one who is called "the lily of the valley and the bright and morning star." No black preacher would dare to "tell the story" without reference to Jesus, because he *is* the gospel story. Without him there is no story to tell and no gospel to celebrate. The centrality of Jesus is so dominant in the black church experience that some scholars have referred to its Christianity as "Jesusology." Although the term "Jesusology" is misleading, it does point to the christological center of black religion and its similarity with Barth's theology.

Also like Barth, the black church regards the Bible as the primary source for knowledge about Jesus and God. It was usually the first book that black slaves learned to read and the one which every black Christian had in his or her home. The Bible is the "good Book," God's true Word to which the people turn for knowledge of God and for guidance on how to live. No preacher would dare preach without a text from the Bible and frequent references to the gospel truth found in it. No Christian can describe the meaning of the "good life" without references to ethics arising out of the Bible. Whatever we say about black religion, it is a religion of the "good Book," and that alone makes it partly compatible with Barth's theology.

Barth's emphasis on the Word of God as preached makes his theology particularly compatible with the black church. Anyone with the slightest knowledge of the black church knows that preaching is one of its most distinctive contributions. Preaching in the black church is the medium through which God tells the divine story of Jesus. In the black church, preaching is understood as not only a human word, not just Reverend So-and-So's word, but primarily, through the work of God's Spirit, the divine Word of grace and judgment to the people. Similarly Barth says: "It is a miracle of revelation and of faith when . . . proclamation to us is not a human volition and execution qualified in some way, but also and primarily and decisively God's own act, when for us [human] language about

God is not only [human] language, but also and primarily and decisively God's own language."[4]

Barth was the main nonblack influence in my writing of *Black Theology and Black Power*. My dependence was considerable; Deotis Roberts and my brother Cecil (among others) thought it excessive. I knew Barth's limitations as I wrote. Scholarly criticism sharpened my awareness, even though I was not in full agreement with my critics. My use of Barth diminished in later books, but I continued to use the work of European theologians when it suited my purposes.

When I began to write my second book, *A Black Theology of Liberation*, I used Barth along with Paul Tillich and Dietrich Bonhoeffer and, in a minor way, Rudolf Bultmann. I did not bother to sort out their differences or to analyze the problem of using them in the constructive development of a black theology. I was merely searching for ingredients to put in my own view of the gospel and the black liberation struggle. Barth, Tillich, Bultmann, Bonhoeffer, and other Europeans I quoted in support of my perspective did not determine what I said. They were merely the tools I appropriated in order to say what I believed was the truth of the gospel as defined by the black experience. What was decisive for my theological perspective was the fact that black people were being shot in the streets of American cities by white policemen. As I saw the world, white racism was the major evil, and its consequence for the lives of black people had to be exposed in the church and society. I did not know Karl Marx well enough to use him in the analysis. I only knew neo-orthodox, liberal, and orthodox theologians of Europe and North America. It seemed to me that liberal theology's view of the Bible, Jesus, and preaching was too much determined by the challenge of the Enlightenment. Black church people would not respond enthusiastically to the historical-critical approach to the Bible, and especially the historical Jesus. Orthodox theology was determined too much by fundamentalism and the literal approach to the Bible. Furthermore, orthodox theologians were often blatant racists. Neo-orthodox theology was the only major school left, and they appeared to take the best and to reject the worst in both liberal and orthodox theologies. Although the death of God theology was a major news item in the 1960s, it was a joke in the black community. Secular theology, as defined by Harvey Cox's *Secular City*, seemed to be a creative analysis of neo-orthodox theology in the direction that I wanted to take black theology. The same was true of Jürgen Moltmann's *Theology of Hope*, a book that was particularly helpful in my initial attempt to relate theology to the struggle for freedom.

Barth was useful because of his central focus on the Bible and Jesus Christ, Tillich for his focus on culture and the human situation, Bultmann for his emphasis on preaching and the present existential situation, and Bonhoeffer for his concern for the concreteness of theology as defined by the ethical demands of politics. They were like a smorgasbord of theologies from which I took what I wanted and left the rest, with Jesus Christ as defined by the Bible and the black experience as my central theological norm. At no point did a European theologian, not even Barth, control what I said about the gospel and the black struggle for freedom. It was the other way around. Jesus as defined by the black experience and the Bible decided how I used European theology. And the explication of Jesus Christ, the Bible and the black experience was decided in the struggle itself and in dialogue with others who had made a similar commitment.

With the decline of NCBC and BMCR in the early 1970s, the black church as the primary context for my theological reflections became increasingly problematic. The United Methodist Church was very large and seemed to have returned to its own white agenda. However, the National Division of the Board of Global Ministries, then under the directorship of Dr. Randolph Nugent, provided several creative contexts for my dialogue with the church on the issues of racism, oppression, and theology. During my sabbatical year (1978-79), I served as a theologian in residence for the National Division and also at Macedonia AME Church in Flushing, New York. In this situation, I had the opportunity to assess my own perspective of

the gospel with the daily work of the church in the local
congregation and in the National Division of the Board of
Global Ministries that serves many congregations.

The decline of NCBC also led many black scholars to organize
the Society for the Study of Black Religion (SSBR) in 1970.
SSBR began to do much of the reflective work that was done by
the Theological Commission of NCBC. But unlike NCBC, it was
devoted almost exclusively to academic matters and often alien
to concerns of the black church. Membership was limited to
seminary- and university-trained persons who were engaged in
teaching. The design of SSBR was similar to the American
Academy of Religion (AAR). The major difference between the
two was that SSBR's members were exclusively black and concerned with black problems, and AAR had primarily white
members and was concerned with white problems. Although I
have been deeply involved in SSBR, I have been disappointed in
its refusal to focus more directly on the problems in the black
church and the issues arising from black people's struggle for
freedom.

In January, 1974, the bishops of the AME Church invited me,
along with Dr. Allen O. Miller (then at Eden Theological
Seminary), to lead a four-day retreat in Galveston, Texas, on the
theme "The Nature and Mission of the Church." It was the first
time since my graduation from Garrett-Northwestern that I had
ever received an invitation to do anything for the AME Church.
Although I was pleased and quite excited about the invitation, I
had to inform the bishops that I would have to say what I
believed to be the truth of the gospel, and it would not be
pleasant for them to hear. If they were not ready to hear harsh
words, then they should ask someone else. They assured me that
I was free to speak on the nature and mission of the church as I
saw it in the Bible and in the history of the AME Church. I will
never forget that occasion, because it was one of the most
creative events in which I have ever participated.

The bishops were serious, and they faced the reality of the
contradiction between the current AME Church, on the one
hand, and the biblical church and the church of Richard Allen,

on the other. They appeared to accept their shortcomings without the slightest defensiveness but always with determination to overcome them. Using the Bible and AME history, I tried to show how unchristian much of the activity of the current AME Church was. I was amazed at the bishops' openness to hear the truth and to search for ways to implement it. Since I knew firsthand the internal workings of the AME denomination, I could be specific regarding the contradictions between the present AME Church and the biblical church. They struggled seriously with the integrity of their Christian identity as I continually emphasized that the chief mission of the church was the liberation of the victims so as to bear witness to God's coming kingdom. Although the contemporary AME Church still refers to Richard Allen as its chief founder, if he were present to see what has been made of his church, he would not recognize it. It has been made a "den of robbers." The process of electing the bishops is a disgrace to human decency. How can anyone be a bishop in the AME Church and not fight against the corruption that is so blatant and pervasive?

As I listened to the bishops struggle with these questions, I concluded that there was much hope for the AME Church. Their struggle was not superficial, for they realized that their identity as the people of God and the church of Richard Allen was at stake. Instead of rejecting my sharp questions, they formally invited me to "come back home" and rejoin the AME Church in order to help bring it back to the Bible. They also invited me to lead another retreat for them the next year. I accepted both invitations with enthusiasm and with the intention of serving the AME Church in the role of a critical theologian.

On the basis of the Bishops' Retreat and a follow-up Connectional Convocation held in Kansas City, Missouri (February 1974), the bishops began to lead the AME Church toward a new self-understanding more consistent with its historical origins. On the theme of "the nature and mission of the church," they declared that their "task is to distinguish what is the distinctive and special mission of the AME Church" which they unequivocally identified with the "deeper needs of black people." They also affirmed the ministry of "liberation and reconciliation" and the need to reflect the acceptance of "blackness" in the worship and life of the church. Another conclusion identified the need to write a distinctive creed, "which speaks to the importance of the African Methodist heritage and that enunciates our concept of personhood." The bishops also took a stand against racism and identified the AME Church with the poor and the oppressed.

Following the Connectional Convocation at Kansas City, preparations began for implementating the conclusions, and plans were made for the second Bishops' Retreat that was to be held at Union Theological Seminary in New York, February 1975. Between the two retreats, I attended many AME meetings. The bishops also requested that I write a working paper on the theology of the AME Church for their second retreat. Returning to the AME Church in the role of a critical theologian was exciting and meaningful. I was certain that the AME Church was ready to move in the direction of a prophetic critique of itself.

The second Bishops' Retreat went well but was not nearly as successful as the first one. The bishops seemed less concerned about the theology and history of the AME Church and more concerned about the politics of the forthcoming General Conference to be held in Atlanta, June 1976. Old pietistic rationalization began to appear, and the bishops seemed much more defensive about the immorality of the institutional operations of the AME Church.

Despite some misgivings regarding the second retreat, I was still optimistic regarding the writing of a series of Black Position Papers that were to define the AME Church's perspective on the gospel and world events. My essay, "God Our Father, Christ Our Redeemer, Man Our Brother: A Theological Interpretation of the AME Church," was adopted as the theological foundation of the other Black Position Papers.[5] Also work began on a credo statement of the AME Church. The series of meetings in which I was involved seemed serious and progressive, but the closer the time of the General Conference approached, the more the politics of the AME Church disrupted our work. Also some prominent AME ministers began to question the church's focus on blackness. In the *AME Christian Recorder*, the then editor, the Reverend A. Lewis Williams, wrote an editorial "Blackness, Let Us Watch It."[6] He was referring to the "working draft" of the credo statement. "I found myself wondering about a creedal statement based on ethnic concerns," he wrote. He contended that creeds are "universal," not ethnic. Williams' comments, as the editor of the most influential AME paper, showed how deep the internalization of white religion had penetrated the minds and hearts of some black ministers. Anyone who has even a little acquaintance with critical independent thinking knows that all human speech is limited by time, including the Bible and the creeds of the early church. It is unfortunate that a person of such a prominent position in the AME Church could be so limited in his theological vision.

On the occasion of the Atlanta 1976 General Conference of the AME Church, I began to realize that I had underestimated the church's resistance to radical change. It is one thing to talk to individual bishops and ministers about the need of the church to identify with the poor and quite another to create the process in which the identification can occur. Many black ministers said about the corruption in the AME Church what white liberals said about racism in their churches and the society. They pointed either to the resistance of other people or to the resistance of the bureaucracy itself. What was clear in all cases was the unwillingness of any prominent AME minister to risk his reputation by challenging the blatant evils in the church. Like white churches, the AME Church and other black churches are good at passing resolutions against racism and other forms of injustice, but seldom do they do anything to implement what they resolve. At the General Conference, I felt completely frustrated and could not believe that any church people could behave so unchristianly.

Of course, I know that all institutions are corrupt, but not all use the Christian label. When an institution claims a Christian identity, then it is open to the sharp theological criticism based on Jesus Christ as witnessed in the Bible. It is, therefore, at the point of the AME Church's *Christian* identity that I am troubled when I think of how the bishops are elected and other church matters are conducted. While I realize that the morality of white churches is worse than black churches, I do not think that this fact can excuse the black churches from their accountability to the gospel as defined by their history. White churches have always been pro-American and against black freedom. But black churches cannot afford to allow their Christian identity to be derived from an identification with America. We must realize, with Langston Hughes, that "America has never been America to me." What did it mean for the 1976 General Conference of the AME Church to find time to hear then candidate for President, Jimmy Carter, but not to find time to assess critically its identity as the people of God? During the entire two-week session, there was hardly any time available for a critical evaluation of the nature and mission of the AME Church.

Accordingly, it seemed that it was time for another sharp critique of black churches similar to the one in *Black Theology and Black Power*. In the context of the Black Theology Project's Conference of Theology in the Americas that was co-sponsored by NCBC (Atlanta 1977), I began my critique in an address entitled "Black Theology and the Black Church: Where Do We Go From Here?"[7] This lecture was followed by an essay "Black Ecumenism and the Liberation Struggle"[8] delivered at Yale University to a conference on the black church, February 1978.

In other lectures, essays, and particularly seminars in black churches, I have been engaged in a critique of the black church. If the black church does not recover its authentic, liberating past, it will not be able to know what to do in the present in order to build a new future. There are many problems which the black church generally and the AME Church in particular need to face.

(1) Black church leaders devote too much time to the organizational operations of their churches. There is hardly any time left for other matters outside of specifically church

business. At least 95 percent of the AME's time and energy is spent on itself: holding meetings and conferences on various aspects of the church, appointing and electing officers, and building and buying church buildings. I have nothing against these institutional matters, but they should be in service to the gospel of Jesus Christ. For any church to devote an inordinate amount of time to itself is to deny Jesus Christ, from whom its Christian identity is derived. As Hugo Assmann has said: "The church cannot be the reason for its own existence." The church's distinctive identity is found not in itself but in the crucified Jesus, whose spirit calls the church into being for service on behalf of victimized people.

(2) By devoting itself to its own organizational routine, the black church tends to accept uncritically white American religion and culture. That is why most black church persons do not know anything about Henry Highland Garnet, Nathaniel Paul, David Walker, and Andrew Bryan. When people lose their historical identity, they have no other alternative but to assume the identity of the group that conquers them. Why do black churches still have pictures of white Christs in their churches? Why do they still reject black images of Christ? Why do they still use images of white boys and girls, men and women in their Sunday school and other educational literature? Is not this a form of self-hate? When our black boys and girls, men and women are being so blatantly dehumanized by *white* oppressors, why do we black Christians use images and symbols that reflect the values of the people that are responsible for our oppression? Unless the black church faces this issue head on, then it does not deserve to be called the church of Jesus Christ.

(3) Related to the easy acceptance of white religion because of a loss of its own identity is the failure of the black church to develop its own theology in creeds, liturgy, and other documents. When Luther and other Europeans separated themselves from Roman Catholicism, the issue was primarily theological. Why then was Richard Allen's and other blacks' separation from the white church any less theological? The lack of a distinctive historical identity led to the disappearance of the

unique theological identity of the black church as well. That was why the AME bishops could say in their Episcopal Salutation (1972 *Discipline*), "Like its Mother Methodism the great urge and passion of the AME Church was not theological but social; not doctrinal but redemptive." The equation of theological identity of the AME Church with white Methodism means that the former has lost its distinct historical identity. If a creative and distinct Christian theology does not arise out of the historical struggle for justice, then from where does it come? The failure to recognize this obvious theological point can only mean that the theological perspective of many black leaders is derived from the dominant culture that thinks of its own particular values as universal.

The absence of a creative theological consciousness has had its impact on theological education in the black church. Most black churches do not support their theological schools, because they do not regard theology as essential to their mission. As they see it, their task is to preach the gospel without critically asking, What is the gospel and how is it related to black life? Black churches tend to assume that everybody knows what the gospel is, even without asking about its primary meaning. Thus there is no genuine self-criticism in the church, no critical theological self-examination. As a result, when new issues emerge in church and society, like feminism and Marxism, black churches are almost always conservative in their response to them. Because there is no genuine theological examination, black churches are helpless in their attempt to create a future for themselves.

(4) One of the most serious problems in the black church is the lack of genuine leadership accountability. I can speak from personal experience with the AME Church. But the problem is not limited to my church; it is found in most black churches. For example, several bishops in the AME Church (during their first retreat in Galveston, Texas) compared the power and authority of their office with that of a white slaveholder. They admitted that many of them had misused their office because of an absence of genuine accountability. As I see it, the accountability of the AME bishops to Jesus Christ as defined by the struggle of

the people for justice is indispensable for the future life of that church.

What has been said of the AME bishops can also be said of prominent pastors in many other black churches. The center of the church's life is often limited to the style and behavior of the pastor. How can the black church be the church of Jesus Christ if its center is located in the pastor?

(5) Another serious weakness of the black church is the absence of a genuine ecumenical vision. To be sure, it is involved in the World Council of Churches, Consultation on Church Union (COCU), and other major white ecumenical bodies in Europe and North America. But since the decline of NCBC, the ecumenical vision of the black churches among themselves seems to have been lost. Why do black churches remain separated from one another when the gospel demands unity and the liberation of black people depends upon it? In my essay "Black Ecumenism and the Liberation Struggle," I pointed to the problem of institutional self-interest as being the chief reason for the ecumenical failure of black churches. They are more interested in their own organizational operations, with their rewards of prestige and financial profit for individual leaders, than they are in the advancement of the total black liberation struggle.

The same selfish interest that separates black denominations also separates men and women, black people in North America from other minorities and from the masses of the Third World countries. There is no doubt that the black church is a sexist church, which is a denial of the gospel. The black church is male dominated, but more than 75 percent of its members are women. With so much talk about feminist theology and the need to develop a gospel that includes all, why is the black church so slow in addressing the separation of black men and women in the church and in society? The answer is obvious: the self-interest of the men, who have most of the power, prevent it.

A similar pattern is found in the black church's relation to other racial minorties in the United States. One would think that the common condition of oppression would bring different races together. But that has not happened because many oppressed people believe the lies that the oppressor promotes about the oppressed. As a black church person, I think black churches could do more in breaking down the barriers that separate them from other minorities than they have done in the past.

When one turns to analyze missionary work in the Third World, the failure of black churches is obvious. We have done very little creative work in Africa, even less in South America, and nothing in Asia. In Africa black churches often adopted similar attitudes toward Africans that were found among white missionaries. Is that really surprising since black churches did not understand themselves as having a different gospel? When white missionaries were challenged by Africans to develop indigenous leadership, black churches did not follow suit. That is why the AMEs still send black American bishops to Africa.

In Latin America and Asia, the AME Church is unknown to the masses of people. When it is realized that there are over sixty million blacks in Latin America (over forty million in Brazil alone), why has the black church failed to make itself known? There are more people in Asia than on any other continent, but the black church is virtually unknown there. It would appear that the same self-interest that sends black American bishops to Africa also impedes the service that the black church could do in Latin America and Asia.

The concerns of the black church should be not in gaining more members for itself but only in liberating the victims wherever they are found. But in order to do that, the black church must divest itself of its preoccupation with itself and become identified exclusively with the interest of Jesus Christ, who is always found among the poor, liberating them from bondage. Can the black church lose itself in order to save itself? Frankly, I do not know, but I hope so!

4
Black Theology and Third World Theologies

Besides the black church and community, nothing has made a greater impact upon the development of my theological and political consciousness than the cultures and theologies of Africa, Asia, and Latin America. This influence can be seen in my teaching at Union Seminary, my travels to the Third World, and my theological writings. No longer is Europe generally and Germany in particular the primary place to look for recent creative theological voices. The eruption of the poor in Asia, Africa, and Latin America has created Third World voices in theology that are radically different from the dominant theologies of Europe and North America. Third World theologians challenge not only the unjust economic and political structures of the world but especially the religious and theological structures that serve as their justification. I believe that no one can do creative theological reflection today without dealing with the impact of those theologians.

When I first began to write about black theology, my concern was limited almost exclusively to the political and social struggle of black people for equality in the United States. In addition, my graduate studies in theology and history, as well as my personal travels, did not include the Third World. Therefore I could not include the peoples of Asia, Africa, and Latin America in my theological perspective, because I had not encountered them either intellectually or existentially.

Of course, I was aware of Africa and the impact that slavery and colonization had had upon black people of the world. I was also aware of the contemporary African struggle for political independence and its connection with the life and writings of W. E. B. DuBois, often referred to as the father of Pan-Africanism. There has always been a strong black nationalist current in the black struggle for justice in the U.S., beginning with Martin Delaney in the nineteenth century, entering the church through Bishop Henry M. Turner, reaching its greatest moment in Marcus Garvey's "back to Africa" movement, and experiencing a profound rebirth in the black consciousness movement in the 1960s. No serious student of black history can ignore the prominent place that Africa has occupied in black thought.

Furthermore, the civil rights movement of the 1950s occurred during the same period as the African movement for political independence, and they influenced each other. Indeed, the rise of Black Power in 1966 included in its political and cultural meanings a concept of black consciousness that embraced black people of the world, especially Africans. The dashiki, natural hair style, and African jewelry were popular cultural manifestations of black North Americans' desire to embrace their African heritage. Black and African studies programs reflected the same desire among black college and university students. Almost every aspect of black life, religious and secular, was affected by the black conciousness movement. "Black is beautiful" became a popular expression, indicating black people's acceptance of themselves as black. When the emphasis on blackness began to focus on an identity that was primarily defined by African life and culture, Afro-Americans began to replace the term "black" with "African" as the most appropriate expression of their identity as a people. By the late 1960s and early 70s, the expression "we are an African people" had become the dominant slogan among black nationalist groups. The movement from "Colored" to "Negro" to "Black" to "African" reflects the search for identity among people whose ancestors were stolen from the continent of Africa.

The search for identity among North Americans of African descent is especially noticeable in the church. Immediately after Stokely Carmichael and other SNCC (Student Non-Violent Coordinating Committee) members proclaimed Black Power as the most appropriate replacement for civil rights and integration (Summer 1966), Black Power was also endorsed by a radical group of ministers who called themselves an ad hoc National Committee of Negro Churchmen. The word "Negro" in their name reflected their close association with the civil rights movement and Martin Luther King, Jr., but their endorsement of Black Power indicated that they intended to separate themselves from King's unqualified acceptance of the concepts of nonviolence and integration. The word "Negro" remained in their name at least until the fall of 1968. By 1969 the word "Black" had replaced "Negro" and the word "Conference" later replaced "Committee," the first change indicating a further movement toward the affirmation of the idea of blackness and the second suggesting their permanent existence as a group. This new breed of churchmen did not wish to promise whites that they would urge blacks to adopt nonviolence while their people were being violently crammed into ghettos of American cities and shot if they expressed any dissatisfaction about their treatment.

Their embracing of the term "Black" instead of "Negro" reflected not only their rejection of the idea of integration but also their movement toward a global view of the struggle for justice. Early NCBC documents, beginning with the July 1966 "Black Power" statement, focused almost exclusively on the domestic problems of race. It is revealing that there is no reference to the war in Vietnam or to colonization and poverty in Africa, Asia, and Latin America. But the "Message to the Churches from Oakland" (1969) indicates that the peoples of Africa, Asia, and Latin America were gradually becoming a part of NCBC's perspective. It was this developing global perspective that caused NCBC to send two representatives to the second assembly of the All-Africa Conference of Churches (AACC) in Abidjan, Ivory Coast, in 1969. Later NCBC's African Commission sponsored (with the Tanzanian Council of Churches) and first formal consultation between black and African theologians and church people.[1]

It is important to note that the perspective of black churches has almost always included a token reference to their African origin. Some Methodist and Baptist churches still retain the term "African" in their names and also send missionaries to the continent. Although NCBC's ecumenical solidarity with African churches attempted to move beyond the missionary approach of traditional black churches, its perspective on the world was largely limited to the fight against racism and did not include an analysis of class and imperialism. The absence of class analysis in the context of U.S. imperialism has meant that their global perspective has been almost exclusively limited to Africa. NCBC has shown some concerns for the Caribbean but less for Latin America, and almost none for Asia.

My perspective on black theology was largely defined by the assets and limitations of the black church, especially NCBC. I began with an exclusive focus on racial injustice in the United States. Later, Africa was incorporated largely because of my involvement in NCBC and also the Society for the Study of Black Religion (SSBR), both of which initiated dialogues with African theologians. But even before my dialogue with Africans, I was severely criticized by several black theologians for failing to include Africa in my theological perspective. The dialogue with Africans, the criticism of black theologians, and the black nationalist proclamation that "we are an African people," led me to ask how Africa's struggle for political independence was connected with black people's struggle for freedom in North America.

However, my development along that line was slow. The difficulty was not intellectual but existential. I did not want to write a black theology that was primarily defined by the interests of black scholars and activists. Some of those interests were alien to my perspective, while others seemed inconsistent with their own stated aims. Some black nationalists, for instance, embraced an African identity of their own making, separating themselves not only from black Americans but also from Africans. Some of them were openly anti-theological and anti-Christian in their analysis of black religion. Even among some black theologians, the interest in Africa seemed to be mainly academic, arising largely from their concern for black studies and African studies programs and from an attraction to secular black nationalist movements. Where was the *theological* imperative in our connection with Africa? What did Africa have to do with Macedonia in Bearden? Because of my commitment to the faith of the black church, I refused to adopt too quickly a black religious nationalism that seemed unconnected with the life-experiences of black church people.

In the midst of such confusion and misdirection, I was hesitant to include Africa in my theological perspective, even though I also knew in the depths of my being that I was more African than European. The issue for me was not whether to include Africa in black theology, but how and in what way should it be included. If including Africa meant excluding the Christian identity in black religion, then I was not prepared to do that. Though human beings are defined by their historical and cultural development, history and culture are not the final determinants of our humanity. History is the place where we struggle to be human, and culture is the tool we develop in order to defend the integrity of our humanity; neither has the final word about who we are. It is at this point that the meaning of Jesus Christ becomes important for Christians. He is the definitive and final word for Christians regarding their humanity.

Jesus Christ was the final norm in my perspective on black theology not because I studied theology at a white seminary;

rather Jesus Christ was made the final norm for black theology because, and only because, he was the final norm for the black church. If black theology, I contended, was not Christian, then it could have only an adversary relationship with the black church. As a black *Christian* theologian, I was often troubled by the seemingly easy way in which black North American theologians' identity with Africa appeared to loosen their identity with the faith of the black church. They began to speak as if African traditional religions could replace Christianity for blacks in North America. African traditional religions are important for Africans and for some North American black scholars whose intellectual interest is focused on Africa; yet one is not genuinely "converted" to a religion apart from a community in which it is celebrated and practiced daily. Where was the community in North America that could bear witness that African traditional religions represented a better way of life for blacks in this country than the Christian faith? Or was I supposed to drop the religion of Macedonia and other black churches merely because I had now visited our African homeland? I began to notice that many black scholars said one thing in an academic setting but another on Sunday morning in a black church. When confronted with these contradictions, some would reply they were actually saying the same thing in both contexts, because both black and African religions were identical in their roots. Black church people may not *know* it, they claimed, but their religion is unquestionably African. The task of the scholar theologian, therefore, is to demonstrate their continuity so that black North Americans can openly affirm their true African identity. Needless to say, I did not share the view that black religion was more African than Christian. Because of my persistence in grounding black theology in the Bible and the black struggle for freedom, and not African traditional religions, I was often sharply criticized by my colleagues.

While I did not switch to my black colleagues' ideas about African traditional religions, they did force me to consider Africa as an important source in my theological perspective. This was the beginning of my serious looking at the world beyond the limitations of the black experience in North America. Later I encountered Asia, Latin America, and the Caribbean through extensive reading and travel. From my encounters with the struggles of the Third World poor, existentially and intellectually, my perspective on the gospel has been enlarged and reinforced. The universal dimension of the gospel was revealed in the particularities of poor people throughout the world. It was this universalism in the gospel that prevented me from elevating the black experience or the African reality to an absolute norm in black theology. While there is no knowledge of Jesus' gospel apart from the particular struggles of the poor for liberation, we must never absolutize a particular struggle (whether black, African, Asian, or Latin) to the exclusion of others. How could I say that the black liberation struggle in the U.S. is a more valid expression of the gospel than the Korean liberation struggle in Japan? Or the struggles of the poor in Latin America? Or the Native American struggle in the U.S.? The list could go on. It was this kind of exclusivism in European theology that had generated liberation theologies in the Third World. Because I firmly believe that the gospel is a message of liberation for the world's poor, I have tried to reflect that theme in my writings about African, Latin, and Asian theologies.[2] In this chapter, I will attempt to analyze the common origin of Black and Third World theologies and the impact of their mutual dialogue upon each other. What were the factors that generated the rise of black and Third World theologies? What are their similarities and differences? These are the questions that will concern us in this chapter.

Origin of Black and Third World Theologies

All Third World theologies began as a reaction to the dominant theologies of Europe and North America. Instead of accepting the prefabricated theologies of their former colonizers, Third World peoples are developing their own theologies, most of which show a special interest in liberation in the sense of poor people's attempt to free themselves from suffering. The focus on liberation is partly a reaction to the missionary emphasis upon spiritual salvation, as if the gospel of Jesus had no interest in the material conditions of people. Almost universally, progressive Third World people began to realize that the Bible is concerned about the salvation of the whole person, including his or her physical well-being. The neglect of the political and economic aspects of the gospel by white missionaries came to be understood as a deliberate cover-up by oppressors so that Third World victims would not challenge the unjust international economic order. As long as Third World peoples believed that the meaning of the gospel is defined by Europe and North America, they could not develop theological perspectives that would challenge their domination by the First World.

The rise of Third World theologies, with their interest in liberation, was directly related to the emergence of national, political movements of liberation in the countries of their origin. When grass-roots people of the Third World began to rebel against the colonial rule by insisting, sometimes through armed revolution, upon democratic rule, theological perspectives also began to develop with a similar focus. In these theologies, liberation was described differently according to the political needs of the people struggling to liberate themselves from foreign domination. Africans began to speak of a distinct African theology with a special interest in the Africanization or indigenization of the gospel so that they would not have to become European in order to be Christians.[3] Latin Americans spoke of theology with an exclusive emphasis on liberation as defined by Marxist class analysis.[4] Asians also used the term "liberation" in defining Asian theology, but they included in its meaning a special focus on their culture as defined by their great religions. They spoke about contextualization instead of indigenization.[5] Although Caribbean people have not developed a distinct theological perspective comparable to Asian, Latin, and African theologies, there are several indications that they also share many of the concerns for liberation as found among other Third World peoples. Perhaps Caribbean theology will be a theology of liberation that will address itself to the issues of imperialism, classism, and racism.[6]

The origin of North American minority theologies is similar to those of the Third World. Black, Asian, Hispanic, and Native North American minorities have begun to develop distinct theologies of liberation in contrast to the white North American theologies that oppress them.[7]

Included among our liberation theologies of North America is also a distinct feminist theology, which seeks to address the evils of sexism. Although feminist theology began among white North American women, some of the aspects of this theology have been adopted by minority women as well.[8] While minority women have not, for the most part, adopted the extreme radical rhetoric of some white women, minority women do realize that their men are not exempted from sexism. Futhermore, minority men have internalized many of the sexist values of the white male culture which defines the woman's place as in the home, thereby limiting her contribution in the struggle for freedom.

The theologies of liberation, despite similar origins, were slow to enter into conversation with one another. They have been so preoccupied with correcting and uncovering the hypocrisy of Euro-American theologies that they have tended to ignore their relationship to one another. Like their colonizers and oppressors, unfortunately, many Third World people do not believe that they have anything intellectually to learn from other oppressed people. Although some Third World people may fight against their white colonizers and oppressors, as is true of liberation theologians, they are not likely to turn to their Third World brothers and sisters on other continents for intellectual resources of liberation. What they know about one another is often determined by white missionaries and other European mediators. This is tragic because missionaries are just as prejudiced against the one Third World people as they are against another. This means that white missionary information is suspect, because they do not intend for Third World people to build a coalition among themselves.

For if Third World people build a coalition in their struggle, then it would be more difficult for Europeans and North Americans to control the Third World. When Third World people become Christians, Europeans and North American whites must convince them that they are the only people who know what Christianity means. Whatever the oppressed attempt to do, the oppressors must convince the victims that they need their help. The control of a people's thinking is an essential element in sociopolitical oppression.

When I first began to write black theology, the first thing white theologians and church people told black people and other Third World people was that there is no such thing as black theology, because theology does not come in colors. What was so amazing was that many blacks rejected black theology because white theologians, missionaries, and preachers said black theology was not "real" theology. Even today there are some Third World and North American black seminaries that offer courses in systematic theology but do not include their own theology and other oppressed peoples' theologies alongside European theologies. Even some North American black theologies are black in color only, *not in thinking,* because they still contend that only Europeans and persons who think like them are "real" systematic theologians. It is very difficult for Third World people to liberate themselves from a dependence on European thought, because we were trained by adherents of European culture and thus have an inordinate admiration of Europeans' intellectual activity. Therefore even when we rebel against Europeans and North American whites, our rebellion is often limited to our negative reactions.

As noted previously, my earlier writings on black theology suffered from this weakness, and my black colleagues have not let me forget it. But I have been struggling to incorporate the experience and culture of the oppressed into the conceptual tools for articulating black theology. For I contend that our rebellion against Europeans should lead to a second step, namely to an affirmation of our own cultural resources as well as those found among other people who have similar experiences of oppression.

As a black theologian of North America, I have emphasized the need for oppressed church people of the world to begin to develop structures of coalition among themselves so that we can start sharing in a common struggle for freedom. In an organization called Theology in the Americas, oppressed Black, Native American, Hispanic, and Asian Christians have begun to consult regarding their common plight of oppression.[9] Also in an international organization called the Ecumenical Association of Third World Theologians, Asians, Africans, Latin Americans, Caribbeans, and oppressed minorities of North America have begun to discuss these issues. It has been within the context of this international Ecumenical Association of Third World Theologians that black theology has developed a dialogue with other Third World theologies. Other contexts for dialogue include the World Council of Churches and the individual efforts of black and Third World theologians to be in conversation with one another. Our conversations together have revealed many similarities and differences, some of which I will seek to analyze in the remainder of this chapter. The primary focus of my analysis will be black theology and the Third World theologies of Asia, Africa, and Latin America.

Black Theologies and Third World Theologies: Some Similarities

Black and Third World theologies agree that the dominant theologies of Europe and North America must be rejected. In order to emphasize their rejection of the white theologies of North America and Europe, black and Third World theologies have universally focused on the word "liberation" as a description of their theological concern. The earliest reference to liberation as the center of the gospel and as a definition of Christian theology occurred among black and Latin American theologians and church people. It is important to note that black and Latin theologians began to use the term "liberation" almost simultaneously but independently of each other. Liberation became the dominant emphasis of black theology from its beginning with my publications on black theology. One year after the publication of my *A Black Theology of Liberation,* the Spanish edition of Gustavo Gutierrez's book, *A Theology of Liberation* (1971), was published. Other black and Latin theologians followed with an emphasis on the same theme.

The theme of liberation is found among Asian and African theologies as well. The common concern of rejecting the dominant theologies of Europe and North America and the emphasis on liberation led Third World theologies to organize the Ecumenical Association of Third World Theologians, whose first assembly was held at Dar es Salaam, Tanzania, in 1976. An account of the meeting was published under the title *The Emergent Gospel.* Since the organizing Assembly in Tanzania, meetings have been held in Ghana (1977), Sri Lanka (1979), and Brazil (1980), with each focusing upon the theology of the continent in which the meeting was held. *African Theology En Route* is a record of the Ghana meeting, and *Asia's Struggle for a Full Humanity* is an account of the Sri Lanka meeting. A record of the Brazil conference, focusing on Latin theology, is called *The Challenge of Basic Christian Communities.* In an effort to lay a foundation for the development of a Third World theology that would be defined by our common struggle for freedom, a New Delhi conference was held, under the theme "The Irruption of the Third World: A Challenge to Theology," in August 1981. When one analyzes the Final Statements of each conference, the rejection of European theology and an affirmation of liberation are common characteristics.[10]

In addition to the rejection of European theology and the affirmation of liberation, black and Third World theologies also stress the need to *reread* the Bible in the light of the struggles of the poor for freedom. They have begun to speak of the "hermeneutical privilege" of the poor, and of God's option for the poor, that is, God's decision to be with the oppressed in times of trouble. The rereading of the Bible in the light of God's option for the poor has led to an emphasis on the Exodus, the prophets, and upon Jesus Christ as the liberator of the poor and the downtrodden.

It has been within the context of our attempt to reread the

Bible that the idea of the "suffering God" has become important in our theological perspective. Although Jürgen Moltmann's writings about the "Crucified God" have been provocative for our theological imagination, as has Luther's distinction between the "theology of glory" and the "theology of the Cross," it has been the actual sufferings of the oppressed in Africa, Asia, and Latin and North America that have been the most decisive in our reflections on the cross of Jesus Christ. As Gustavo Gutierrez has said, "We cannot speak of the death of Jesus until we speak of the real death of people." For in the deaths of the poor of the world is found the suffering and even the death of God. The political implications of Luther's insight on this point are distorted by his unfortunate emphasis on the two kingdoms. Modern-day Lutheran scholars are even worse, because they appear to turn the cross of Jesus into a theological idea, completely unrelated to the concrete historical struggles of the oppressed for freedom. For most Lutheran scholars, the theology of the cross is a theological concept to be contrasted with philosophical and metaphysical speculation. It is a way of making a distinction between justification by grace through faith and justification by the works of reason.

But when the poor of the Third World and of North America read of Christ's passion, they do not view it as a theological idea but as God's suffering solidarity with the victims of the world. Jesus' cross is God's election of the poor by taking their pain and suffering upon the divine person. This is what Third World theologians mean when they say that "God is Black," "God is Red," "God is Rice," and use other expressions that are strange when compared to the metaphysical reflections of Europeans. This apparently crude, anthropomorphic way of speaking of God is the Third World theologian's way of concretizing Paul's saying that "God chose what is foolish in the world to shame the wise, God chose what is weak in the world to shame the strong, God chose what is low and despised in the world, even the things that are not, to bring to nothing the things that are" (I Corinthians 1:27-28 RSV).

Another common emphasis among black and Third World

theologians is their affirmation of their own cultural traditions. If the sufferings of God are revealed in the sufferings of the oppressed, then it follows that theology cannot achieve its Christian identity apart from a systematic and critical reflection upon the history and culture of the victims of oppression. When this theological insight impressed itself upon our consciousness, we Third World theologians began to realize that we have been miseducated. In fact, European and North American theologians and missionaries have stifled the indigenous development of theological perspectives of Third World peoples by teaching them that their own cultural traditions are not an appropriate source for an interpretation of the Christian gospel. Europeans and white North Americans taught us that the Western theological tradition, as defined by Augustine, Aquinas, Luther, Calvin, and Wesley, is the essential source for a knowledge of the Christian past. When black and Third World theologians began to concentrate on distinct black, African, Asian, and Latin theologies, they also realized that their own historical and cultural traditions are far more important for an analysis of the gospel than are the Western traditions which participated in their enslavement. African traditional religions and the African Independent Churches played a vital role in the development of African theology. The black spirituals, blues, and folklore, as well as radical nineteenth-century black freedom fighters, played a special role in the rise of black theology. The major religions of Asia, including Hinduism and Buddhism, are being integrated into the current shape of Asian theology. In Latin American theology, the most Western of all liberation theologies, some theologians have also turned to their own cultural history for guidance and inspiration. All Third World theologians realize that the people responsible for our enslavement are not likely to provide the resources for our freedom. If oppressed peoples are to be liberated, they must themselves create the means for it to happen.

The focus on our culture in the light of our liberation struggle has led to an emphasis upon *praxis* as the context out of which Christian theology develops. Action and thought are related. To know the truth is to do the truth, that is, to make happen in history what is confessed in church. All proponents of liberation theology contend that people are not poor by accident. They are *made* poor by the rich and powerful few. This means that to do liberation theology, one must make a commitment, an option for the poor and against those who are responsible for their poverty. Because liberation theology is not simply something to be learned and taught in colleges and seminaries but to be created only in the struggles of the poor, social analysis becomes a critical component of all forms of liberation theology. How can we participate in the liberation of the poor from oppression if we do not know *who* the poor are and *why* they live in poverty? Social analysis is a tool that helps us to know why the social, economic, and political orders are arranged as they are. It enables us to know who benefits from the present status quo. Unlike European and North American theology, whose conversation partner is philosophy, liberation theologians converse with sociology. Agreeing with Karl Marx's eleventh thesis on Feuerbach, they say: "The philosophers have only interpreted the world in various ways; the point however is to change it." In the Ecumenical Association of Third World Theologians and in other contexts, black and other Third World theologians have been searching for ways in which they can change the world together.

In our use of the tools of the social sciences for an analysis of the social, political, and economic structures that dehumanize the poor, Third World theologians almost universally endorse democratic socialism and condemn monopoly capitalism. When we speak of democratic socialism, we do not mean the system of Soviet Russia, eastern European nations, or any other so-called socialist country under the influence of the Soviet Union. Socialism by definition means democracy, and the USSR is not a political democracy. Many Third World people refer to Russia as an example of state capitalism.

Although there are no perfect examples of our socialist vision, its authenticity is based upon the struggles of the poor in the Third World who believe that there is no reason why the present unjust order must continue to exist. And the struggles of people in Zimbabwe, Nicaragua, and other Third World countries symbolize the partial realization of our socialist vision.

For what we do know is that monopoly capitalism is evil and must be opposed. Latin American liberation theologians have taken the lead in condemning and exposing the international capitalism of the USA and Europe, and their voices have been joined by Asians, Africans, Caribbeans, and Third World theologians in the United States. Our conversations together have enlarged our vision and enabled us to analyze more clearly the complexity of the international operation of monopoly capitalism.

While Africans, Asians, and Black North Americans have emphasized the role of culture in the bestowal of identity in the struggle of freedom, we also see more clearly now the importance of Marxism and the place of class analysis in doing theology. Both race and class analyses are important, and their importance is reflected in our support of each other.

Black Theology and Third World Theologies: Some Differences

Although black and Third World theologies share many common concerns, they are not identical. The differences between black theology and Third World theologies in Africa, Asia and Latin America can be classified in two general areas. There are differences that separate us, and there are others that complement and enlarge our liberation perspectives. Both kinds of differences are present in black theology's relationship with African, Latin American, and Asian theologies.

The two main focuses, around which our differences have occurred, are sociopolitical liberation, on the one hand, and cultural liberation, on the other. In our dialogue with African theologians, black theologians have placed more emphasis on sociopolitical liberation, and Africans have stressed cultural liberation. In each of our meetings, Africans have shied away from the term "liberation," because they say that the gospel is not political. It is not an ideology of the oppressed. Some have even said that the gospel is concerned about all, the rich and the poor alike. In place of "liberation," Africans often prefer the terms "Africanization" and "indigenization," because they locate the problem at the point of culture and not politics. But black theologians have been adamant in their insistence that the God of the Bible is a political God who has identified divine righteousness with the bodily liberation of the poor. The differences between African and black theologians on this point have led some African theologians, like John Mbiti, to say that African and black theologies have nothing in common with each other. But the presence of black theology in southern Africa has rendered Mbiti's statement problematic. Desmund Tutu, the present director of the South African Council of Churches, says that black and African theologies are soulmates and not antagonists. A similar point has been made by the black Lutheran Bishop Monas Buthelezi.[11]

The concern of North American black theologians has not been to *reduce* theology and the gospel to blackness or political liberation. Like our African brothers and sisters, we believe that there is a spiritual ingredient in the gospel that transcends the material conditions of people. What we reject is the tendency, among some African theologians, to limit the gospel and theology to a spirituality that has not been carved out of the concrete sufferings of the poor who are engaged in political liberation. When the sufferings of the poor are individualized or privatized, it becomes possible to identify their sufferings with God without challenging the existing sociopolitical arrangements responsible for their suffering. The idea of God's suffering and Jesus' cross become mere intellectual, theological concepts completely unrelated to the actual material conditions of the poor. This is precisely Miguez Bonino's and other Latin theologians' critique of Jürgen Moltmann's writings about the "Crucified God."[12] A much more severe critique can be made of modern-day Lutheran reflections upon Martin Luther's theology of the cross. Even some liberation theologians would make the same critique against Martin Luther because of his failure to extend his theological analysis of the cross to society.

Whether it is Moltmann's Crucified God, Luther's theology of the cross, or African theology's theme of indigenization, the question of the sociopolitical ingredient of the gospel must be faced head on. This has been and still is black theologians' concern in our dialogue with African theologians.

In black theologians' dialogue with Latin American liberation theology the opposite has taken place when compared with our dialogue with Africans. The main question has been: What is the relation between race and class oppression? Because Latin Americans are Marxists, they naturally emphasize class oppression, and almost exclude race oppression. Since black theologians live in the white racist society of North America, with a heritage of two hundred fifty years of slavery and over a hundred years of white capitalist oppression, it is not likely that we will ignore cultural oppression as defined by white racism.

Unfortunately, black theologians have not always been sensitive to class oppression or the role of U.S. imperialism in relation to the Third World. Sometimes we have given the impression that all we want is an equal piece of the North American capitalist pie. Therefore Latin Americans have rightly asked about a social analysis in our theology that criticizes capitalism. In this dialogue with Latin theologians, we have come to realize the importance of Marxism as a tool for social analysis.

As Latin Americans have pushed us on the issue of class analysis, we have pressed them on the importance of race analysis. Like black theologians on Marxism, Latin theologians have not embraced race analysis enthusiastically. Our dialogue began in 1973, and we have struggled with the issue of race versus class since that time. Although the tensions between us have been high, we have learned a lot from each other and intend to carry on the dialogue.

It is revealing to note the changing dynamics and emphases in black theology in its dialogue with African and Latin American theologies. With Africans, we black theologians often appear very "political" in our view of theology, and Africans are more "cultural" and "spiritual." In our conversations with the Latins, black theologians seem very "cultural" and "spiritual," and the Latins appear to reduce theology to "politics." The reason for these changes in dynamics and emphases is partly due to the way we read the Bible and analyze the gospel with our respective situations in view. Another reason is our limited knowledge of each other's situation and the role of our theologies in our struggles of liberation. Sometimes we try to impose our particular theology upon another's situation. The issue is whether our theological perspectives have achieved and still retain their identity out of the struggles of the poor. For I contend that any theological perspective that does not remain committed to the liberation of the victims cannot be Christian. It does not matter on what continent a theology may be found. What is crucial is *who* it represents: the poor or the rich, the black or the white, the First or the Third World?

There has been less dialogue, and almost no conflict between black and Asian theologians. Asians do not know much about black people, and neither do we know much about Asians. The differences in culture and also in geographical distance are so great that we seldom have much to say to each other. This situation began to change when I was invited in 1975 by the Korean Christian Church in Japan to lead a three-week workshop on the theme "The Church Struggling for the Liberation of the People." Since 1975, I have returned to Japan and South Korea several times. Black theologians have met several Asian theologians in the Ecumenical Association of Third World Theologians and found that we have many differences and similarities that complement each other.

Important for my perspective on Asia have been my colleague Kosuke Koyama and my friend Premier Niles of the Christian Conference of Asia, who have done much to teach me about Asian theology. In addition to Koyama and Niles, I must also mention Asian students who have been in my classes at Union Seminary. Their presentation of the Asian reality and their commitment to participate in the struggle to liberate the oppressed on that continent have done much to illuminate my perspective on Asian theology. Like black theology, their perspectives on Asian theology seek to bring together in dialectical tension the commitment to cultural identity and sociopolitical liberation. As I have suggested in my discussion of African and Latin theologies, each seems to be in danger of minimizing one side: the Africans sociopolitical liberation and the Latins cultural liberation. In Asian theology, there is a recognition of the importance of both of these elements. My perspective on black theology has endeavored to recognize both elements as well.

Because our differences and similarities seem to complement each other's perspective, black and Asian theologians have begun to discuss the possibility of a dialogue with each other outside of the Ecumenical Association of Third World Theologians. Preman Niles of the Commission on Theological Concerns of the Christian Conference of Asia has explored this possibility among Asian Christians, and I have done a similar exploration within the context of the Black Theology Project of Theology in the Americas. No dates or agenda for our dialogue have been decided. But each side is anxious to initiate it, because we believe that we will have much to learn from each other.

Because blacks and Asians have had few conflicts in our dialogue, we have been able to transport this experience of mutual support to our respective dialogues with Africans and Latin Americans. Why should we fight each other when we have so much to lose in our division and to gain in our unity? Asians and blacks seem to recognize that point in our theological conversations, and this recognition has enabled us to move to a deeper understanding of each other's struggles.

On the basis of Third World theologians' dialogues together, it is clear to us all that the future of each of our theologies is found in our struggles together. I am firmly convinced that black theology must not limit itself to the race struggle in the United States but must find ways to join in solidarity with the struggles of the poor in the Third World. The universal dimensions of the gospel message require that we struggle not only for ourselves but for all. For there can be no freedom for any one of us until all of us are free. Any theology that falls short of this universal vision is not Christian and thus cannot be identified with the man Jesus who died on the cross and was resurrected so that everyone might be liberated into God's coming kingdom.

5
Black Theology, Feminism, and Marxism

From the time of my childhood to the present, the problem of white racism has been my primary concern, emotionally and intellectually. It influenced my vocational choice for the ministry and defined my intellectual focus in theology. Until the early 1970s, I was thoroughly convinced that racism was the central problem in the world and that its elimination should be regarded as the primary concern of all people, especially those who claim a Christian identity.

It was not until I began to travel to Asia, Africa, and Latin America to read and to talk with Third World and feminist theologians that I also began to recognize the limitations of my early exclusive focus on racism. While I never assumed that blacks in the United States were the only victims of oppression, I did think that the most obvious and severe oppression stemmed from the racial attitudes of whites. The problems of classism and sexism, though present vaguely in my mind, did not appear to warrant the same attention as racism. My early conflicts with Latin American and white feminist theologians were partly due to this false assumption on my part. (Many Latin Americans and white feminist theologians made a similar error in relation to classism and sexism, thereby enhancing our failure to talk creatively with each other.)

While I still think that racism is and must remain the chief focus of my theological and political endeavors, I no longer regard it as the only problem or even the primary contradiction in the world today. Racism is one among many problems, though perhaps the most visible, existing along with sexism, classism, and imperialism. The complexity of the world is such that elevating one of these problems to first priority does not serve to eliminate any of them. It is to be expected that persons who are the victims of any injustice make their entry into the struggle for freedom at the point where it hurts them the most. But that focus should not be allowed to blind them to other manifestations of injustice as well as their interrelation with each other. When I seriously considered the world from the vantage point of other people's experiences, I learned something not only about the uniqueness of their struggles, but also, and perhaps more importantly, about the complexity of racism as well. Racism, classism, sexism, and imperialism are interconnected, and none can be correctly understood and eventually defeated without simultaneous attention to the others. Furthermore, each of these "isms" is related to others, that is, ageism, militarism, anti-Semitism, etc. Unfortunately, blacks, women, and other victims have not always assumed the interrelations of human oppression and thus have often been enemies rather than allies. In this final chapter I want to focus on the impact of feminism and Marxism on my theological and political perspective.

Black Theology and Feminist Theology

When I began writing about black theology, the problem of sexism was not a part of my theological consciousness. When it was raised by others, I rejected it as a joke or as an intrusion upon the legitimate struggle of black people to eliminate racism. I had assumed that the rise of women's liberation was a white trick to distract from the injustice being committed by whites against blacks. As a Southern black, I could not forget the role that white women played in the lynching of black men. The lynching of Emmett Till of Chicago, a fourteen-year-old, for allegedly whistling at a white woman in Money, Mississippi (1955), was one of the most publicized events during my youth. I can remember the fear that many black men experienced while in the vicinity of a white woman, because her word alone could get a person lynched, legally electrocuted, or confined to prison for life. The rise of contemporary feminism and its emphasis on rape seemed to be another version of white racism, not too much different from its earlier manifestation in lynching. How could white women expect black people to be concerned about their fear of rape when so many black men have been lynched for just glancing in their direction? To speak about the contemporary white woman's experience of being raped, without a sustained examination of the past black experience of lynching, appeared to be a white maneuver for avoiding an encounter with their own racism.

Furthermore, what about the rape of black women by white men? The different shades of color among black people are constant reminders of the helplessness of both black women and men in the face of white males' violation of black women's bodies. In the history of the United States, the most conspicuous and helpless victims of rape have been black women, not white women, and yet that racial-sexual problem receives such a low priority in the language and activity of white advocates of women's liberation. Since the women's liberation movement was dominated by whites, and thereby ignored much of the special suffering of black women, I concluded that feminism was white people's way of minimizing the racial suffering of black people. It did not occur to me to be self-critical by looking beyond the superficial elements of feminism to the depth of the real issue. Unfortunately, my early reflections on women's liberation was so completely controlled by black males' fears that I could not think straight regarding the complexity of the problem. It was easy for me to say that if white women are oppressed by their men, it is not the fault of black men. We black men certainly are not oppressing white women.

My education on the women's liberation movement began at Union Seminary. The power and influence of white women's at Union made it very difficult for anyone to ignore the legitimate claims of feminism. As a member of the Union community, serving in the role of a teacher, I could not say that women's liberation was merely a white problem and not of any concern for blacks, if I expected to be an effective teacher of *all* students, regardless of color and sex. If I expected white students and professors to listen to the legitimate demands of black theology, then must not I, as a black man, listen to the legitimate demands of feminist theology, even if it is being written exclusively by white women? It became very clear to me that I could not be an effective teacher of anything if I ignored or dismissed with a laugh the hurts and pains of nearly half of the Union community.

So my first step in an openness to feminism was the recognition of its legitimacy within the context of Union in particular and the white community generally. If black people are going to function effectively in a white context, then they must respond creatively to the hurts of all, even if some people's hurts seem very minor when compared with the oppression of blacks. When people make jokes out of someone else's pain, it is an insult to the humanity of all and thus cannot be tolerated. It does not matter how things appear from my vantage point, it is not legitimate for me to make my experience the final criterion for judging the nature and extent of somebody else's suffering. If I have not been a victim of sexism, how do I know that the pain of racism is greater than the one arising from sexism?

While white women forced me to consider the problem of sexism in a white context, black women forced me to face the reality of sexism in the black community. Many black women contended that their silence on sexism did not mean that it was absent in the black community, but only that they did not wish to divide black men and women in the struggle against racism. Black women's silence began to end at Union and other places, because black men misused their silence by refusing to even consider that sexism was a real problem in the black community. Black men continued to claim that "black women have always been free." As I listened to black women articulate their pain, and as I observed the insensitive responses of black men, it became existentially clear to me that sexism was a black problem too.

I could understand why black men might dismiss the arguments of white women regarding the injustice of sexism. There is so much black pain involved in the history of black male and white female relations that it is quite difficult to give proper attention to all dimensions in a balanced and fair way. But how could I explain a similar response of black men when the problem is raised by black women? Black men are often more insensitive and rude toward black women feminists than they are toward white women. I have heard black women express their legitimate demands in black caucuses, churches, and the community as a whole. But black men often ignore them or treat their pain as a laughing matter. Very few men listen sensitively and respond in an effort to heal their pain by eliminating the evils of sexism. Even if black men do not agree with the whole of black feminists' analysis of sexism in the black community, we are still obligated to listen sensitively to black feminists if we expect to hold the community together in the struggle for freedom. There will be no freedom for any one of us until all of us are free.

The insensitive response of black men made me realize that the problem of sexism was much deeper in the black community than I ever anticipated. No one has brought the issue of sexism in the black community to the attention of the American public more provocatively than Ntozake Shange's Broadway play *For Colored Girls* . . . and Michele Wallace's book *Black Macho and the Myth of the Superwoman*. Regardless of what anyone thinks about the truth of the two statements or the motives behind the white media for promoting them, Shange and Wallace helped to rid black males of the assumption that feminism is an exclusively white concern. It became very clear to me that we black men, in church and society, had better face the painful consequences of our sexist practices or be consumed by the revolution our sisters are making.

It is not for me to say whether my change in consciousness has had any noticeable consequences in my relations with women in my private and public life. There are three females in our family and three males. Sandra and I are the parents, Robynn and Krystal are our daughters and Michael and Charles are our sons. Sandra, Robynn, and Krystal have helped Michael, Charles, and me to respect the meaning of a genuinely liberated family.

The women of Union and elsewhere, especially black, are the best judges regarding my openness to feminist issues. I have tried to listen and to learn from my sisters and have attempted to implement the consequences of my listening and learning in what I teach, write, and do. The rise of a black feminist theology, with the prominent voices of Jacquelyn Grant and Pauli Murray, has done much to teach black men regarding the urgency of black women's liberation in Black Theology and the church. The section on "Black Theology and Black Women" in *Black Theology: A Documentary History* (Wilmore and Cone, eds.) reflects my attempt to introduce black feminist theology in the context of the seminary and the church.

What does black feminist theology mean for the church and theology? This is an important and complex question with many dimensions in it. As I listen to black feminist theologians and read their literature, they appear to be developing a new comprehensive way of thinking about theology, church, and society. While black male theologians focus almost exclusively on racism, white feminists focus primarily on sexism, and Third World theologians or Latin Americans concern themselves with classism, black women are seeking to combine the issues of race, sex, and class, because they are affected deeply by each. It is too early to say what the exact characteristics of black feminist theology will be because it is still in the process of development. What is certain is that it will not be mere duplication of the black

theology of black male theologians or of the feminist theology of
white females. Emerging black feminist theologians seem to be
saying that since all theologies arise out of human experiences,
they must develop a black feminist theology out of the unique
experience of poor black women.

In both black theology and the black church, black feminist
theology offers a radical challenge to the accepted black male
ways of saying and doing things. Black feminists insist that our
language about God which refers to the divine in exclusively
male terms must change in order to reflect the image of God in
black women. The same is true for our language about "man."
To think of God and humanity in exclusive male terms (i.e., God
as "he," and "man" as male and female) reflects a patriarchal
tradition that denies the full humanity of women. Masculine
language in religion and theology serves as theological
justification for the subordination of women in church and
society. In rejecting the patriarchal language of black religion,
black women seem to be agreeing with white feminist
theologians who have made the same point in the theology of
white males. In secular society and the church, black feminists
have challenged black males' easy acceptance of white males'
definition of the place of the woman. According to Frances
Beale, the black man "sees the system for what it is for the most
part, but where he rejects its values on many issues, when it
comes to women, he seems to take his guidelines from the pages
of the *Ladies Home Journal*."[1] And in a similar vein Anna Cooper
says, "While our Black men seem thoroughly abreast of the
times on every subject, when they strike the women question
they drop back into sixteenth century logic."[2] It is this
"sixteenth-century logic" that Jacquelyn Grant exposes with her
penetrating questions and comments.

> How can a white society characterized by black enslavement,
> colonialism, and imperialism provide the normative conception of
> women for black society? How can the sphere of the woman, as
> defined by White men, be free from the evils and oppressions that
> are found in the White society? The important point is that in

matters relative to the relationship between the sexes, Black men have accepted without question the patriarchal structures of the White society as normative for the black community. . . . Many Black women are enraged as they listen to liberated Black men speak about the "place of women" in words and phrases similar to those of the very White oppressors they condemn.[3]

Black males do not like to think of themselves as being similar to racist white men. That is why they would like to dismiss the argument of black women by refusing to discuss the matter with an openness to hear the truth. It is so easy for black men to say that black feminists have been influenced and told what to say by white feminists. Since sexism means that the victim cannot think, black men disclose their assumption in this regard by attributing the thought of black women to "outside white agitators." Such a person only reinforces black men's identity with white men, since the same thing was said of them by whites in the Black Power and civil rights movements.

Some black men claim that there is no oppression of women in the black church. Such a statement sounds like white people saying that there is no racism in the white church. As a black male theologian, I know that the black woman's experience is not adequately reflected in black theology. Most of us have not even thought about the unique suffering of black women. We have not allowed ourselves to be taught by black women so that our theological reflections can more adequately reflect the whole black community. If black women represent nearly 75 percent of the black church membership, does it not follow that the same percentage should be present in the leadership of the church? In the AME Church, for example, why are there no women bishops, general officers, presidents of major colleges, or pastors in the major churches? A similar point can be made about other black denominations. Why have black theologians been silent on this point when we have been relentless in our critique of the racist practices of the white churches? I do not see how we can keep our credibility as "liberation" theologians and remain so unliberated in our dealing with the question of sexism. Nearly all black theologians have either ignored sexism completely or have made such irrelevant comments on it that silence would have been preferable.

In view of the silence of black theologians on the question of sexism, it is not surprising that the black churches seem to be unaware that a problem exists. The subordination of women in the black church is so obvious that I sometimes wonder why any argument is needed to demonstrate it. But women's subordination is taken so much for granted by men and women in the black church that it is difficult for black feminists to address the issue of sexism. When the issue is addressed to black pastors and bishops, their response is often reminiscent of the white responses to subordination of blacks. "The women like it that way," or "women don't want women pastors." When I point out that many whites said the same thing about blacks, black male ministers usually reject the comparison as inappropriate, insisting that black women really *do* like the role they play in the church whereas blacks did not really want to be subordinate but had no alternative. Regardless of what black male ministers claim, their reasoning is very similar to white people's argument for keeping blacks oppressed. No group gives up power freely. Black ministers use all available intellectual and religious resources, including twisted biblical interpretations reminiscent of slaveowners' sermons, in order to justify their privileged position.

I think that black men need to realize that our failure to listen openly with the intention of eliminating the injustice of sexism will create a war between our sisters and us. If we do not listen and change the church and society so as to reflect the full humanity of our sisters, then what alternative do our sisters have except to fight us as their enemies? They cannot and should not accept our claim that "we love them" and that "we are brothers and sisters" if our treatment of them fails to recognize their humanity in ways that they define.

A fight between black men and women will lead to an ineffective struggle against racism. The burden of the responsibility for black unity lies primarily with black men. If black women desert us for the larger feminist movement, we have only ourselves to blame, because they have informed us of their pain but we seem to be too stubborn to listen. We black men need to ask: What kind of society do we wish to create? Do we want a genuinely new society or just the right to replace white men with black men? If we say that we want a genuinely new society, what then will the society look like? Will it be a society without racism and sexism? Will we seek to create a society that has space for the humanity of all? If we answer in the affirmative, then we had better seek to eliminate sexism in the black community or our action will deny our words.

Black Theology and Marxism

Like feminism, Marxism was not a part of my political and theological consciousness when I first began to write about black theology. My introduction to Marx came with my encounter with Third World theologians, especially Latin American liberation theologians. They were strong advocates of class analysis in their writings and also in my personal encounters with them. As with feminism, my first response was to ignore the problem of class, because race appeared to be the most dominant manifestation of injustice in the United States. Because I had not traveled much outside the United States, I was suspicious of Latin Americans, since they were white, and since white North Americans seemed to welcome Latin American liberation theology but ignored black theology. I was also troubled because many Latin Americans said that there was no color problem on their continent. How could that be, I asked, when there are more black people in South America than North America, and yet there are no blacks in your group of liberation theologians? Many of these reservations have been overcome in subsequent dialogues. In particular Latin Americans helped us to realize the importance of Marxism as a tool of social analysis. Also, democratic socialism appears to be a more human alternative to monopoly capitalism.

The encounter with Marxism in my dialogue with Third World theologians forced me to investigate the history of

Marxism and socialism in the United States. It is one thing to talk about Marx's ideas in *The Grundrisse* and *Capital* but quite another to ask what has been the relationship between the black church and Marxism in the United States. It is one thing to talk about Marxism in Europe or even the Third World, but quite another to locate its historical meaning in the North American black community. Has there been much contact between Marxists and black church people? What have been their attitudes toward each other? Before I could decide my own attitude toward marxism, I had to examine the past relationship of Marxists and black church people. Words about freedom and equality are often deceiving in books. The only way one can know what people mean by the words they use is to observe what the words cause them to do. Since I had been forced to connect meaning with action in my critique of white Christians, I thought it would be wise to apply the same principle to white Marxists. In this concluding section, I wish to analyze briefly the historical relationship of the black church and Marxism and thereby lay a foundation for a new dialogue.

The black church and Marxism have emerged on the North American continent from separate historical paths and thus have encountered each other only rarely. Marxism is European in origin and was imported into the United States in 1851 by Joseph Weydemeyer, a friend of Karl Marx. The black church is both African and European in origin. It was created during the late eighteenth and early nineteenth centuries when black people refused to accept slavery and racial oppression as consistent with the gospel of Jesus Christ. During the early period of their existence in North America, there was virtually no contact between black churches and Marxists. Both were preoccupied with their own immediate projects, which were sharply contradicted by the current structures of American capitalism. The primary historical project of Marxists was defined in terms of the destruction of capitalism and the establishment of a socialist society in which the means of production would be owned by the people rather than by an elite ruling class. The primary historical project of the black church was defined as preaching and living the gospel of Jesus in order to receive both the gift of eternal life and the courage to fight against injustice in this world, especially as represented in slavery and racism.

The different histories of the black church and Marxism as well as their different perspectives on the human condition confirmed their separateness in society and thus laid the foundation for their misunderstanding of each other. Because both the black church and Marxism have been marginal in American society, they have been preoccupied with their own survival and have taken little notice of each other. However, to the extent that Marxists and other socialists have been concerned historically with the black community, they have almost always encountered the black church, because the church has been, and to a large degree still is, the most important institution in our community. Similarly, to the extent that black church people have been concerned with creating a completely new society, they have looked in the direction of Marxism. Although the socialist tradition among black church people is small, it is still present, and we black theologians and historians should rediscover it in order to enhance our vision of liberation.

The lack of contact between black church people and Marxists has resulted in distorted views of each other's perspectives. They only know each other from a distance and usually only through the white capitalist media. While each group rejects what their mutual enemy says about them, they seem to accept readily what is said about the other. As far as I know, there have not been many occasions in which Marxist-socialists and black Christians have come together for dialogue looking toward doing some things together to make this society more humane. If black Christians and Marxists expect to initiate a creative dialogue it would be wise to acknowledge the sharp differences in our perspectives but to avoid stressing the minor aspects of our viewpoints. We must be keenly aware of our history in relation to each other so we can build on our strengths and avoid our past mistakes.

Marxism and the Black Church: Historic Attitudes

In the history of relations between black church people and Marxists, we can easily identify three attitudes: indifference, hostility, and mutual support. The most frequent of these has been indifference. In 1911 Thomas Potter, a black socialist from Patterson, New Jersey, wrote: "Let me say in the most emphatic terms that if there is one blot on the record of the Socialist party, it is that of its utter apathy and indifference toward the negro."[4]

Mutual indifference can be seen by the absence of references to each other in their respective expressions of radicalism in the United States. A black person finds it strange that in books on the history of socialism there are few if any references to black radicalism in the United States. The only period in which a few comments are made is in connection with the civil rights and Black Power movements of the 1960s. It is as if black radicalism does not exist for white socialists until the appearance of Martin Luther King, Jr., and Stokely Carmichael. White socialists seem not to know or care about the radicalism of black church people during the nineteenth and early twentieth centuries. A similar invisibility obscures early black socialists, like Peter Clark and the Reverend George Washington Woodbey.

Peter Clark, a principal and teacher from Cincinnati, Ohio, was the first black to declare himself a socialist. "In 1878, he was chosen as a member of the National Executive Committee of the newly formed Socialist Labor Party," but had to resign a year later, because "the welfare of the Negro [was his] controlling motive."[5] The Socialist Labor Party completely ignored the situation of blacks during the late nineteenth century, and the same is true of other socialist groups, including the Socialist Party, organized in 1901.

The Reverend George Washington Woodbey was a member of the Socialist Party, attending the national conventions in 1904 and 1908. In 1908 he was nominated but rejected by the convention as Eugene Debs' running mate in that year's presidential elections. He wrote several books reconciling socialism and Christianity, including *What to Do and How to Do It or Socialism vs. Capitalism* and *The Bible and Socialism: A Conversation Between Two Preachers.*[6]

Unfortunately black socialists are invisible in the histories of socialism written by white intellectuals. Such works as Michael Harrington, *Socialism,*[7] and Daniel Bell, *Marxian Socialism in the United States,*[8] have almost no references to black people's involvement in the socialist movement. Although James Weinstein, in *The Decline of Socialism in America* and *Ambiguous Legacy,*[9] devoted a few pages to blacks in each book, it is quite clear that black people's relation to socialism is not an integral part of his analysis. The conspicuous absence of any reference to the importance of black presence in the Socialist Party or to black radicalism outside the socialist movement can only mean that most white socialists themselves are indifferent to the black struggle for liberation as defined by black people.[10] Anyone interested in why more black people are not socialists should read Philip Foner's *American Socialism and Black Americans.*[11] The socialists' history in America in relation to black people (to quote Engels in another connection) "proves how useless is a platform—for the most part theoretically correct—if it is unable to get in contact with the actual needs of the people."[12] It was the indifference of the Socialist Party to racism that made W. E. B. DuBois ambivalent about his commitment to the party, even though he clearly believed that socialism provided a better social arrangement than capitalism. As early as 1913, DuBois said, "The Negro problem is the great test of the American socialist."[13] In succeeding years white socialists, along with the rest of white society, failed that test. Many socialists, like white Christians, seem to be unaware that there is a serious credibility problem as they are analyzed from a black viewpoint. Like white Christians who appear to be white first and Christian second, white socialists also seem to be white first and socialists second. Such an identity will always present difficult problems in the context of dialogue with black people.

The indifference of socialism toward the black church is mirrored in the indifference of the black church toward socialism. There were black preachers who became advocates of socialism, but either such advocacy remained on the periphery of their message or the preachers themselves remained on the periphery of the black church. In 1896 Reverdy C. Ransom, later a bishop in the AME Church, wrote an article entitled "The Negro and Socialism" in which he advocated socialism. He said that when the "Negro comes to realize that socialism offers him freedom of opportunity to cooperate with all people upon terms of equality in every avenue of life, he will not be slow to accept his social emancipation."[14] During the 1890s *The Christian Recorder* and the *AME Church Review* carried on a dialogue on the strengths and the weaknesses of socialism, with the writers of the *Recorder* rejecting socialism and the writers of the *Review* supporting it. But even the black ministers who supported socialism did not view socialism as central to their perspective on the gospel.

The same is true of black preachers and theologians today. They are indifferent toward socialism, because they know little about it, and because they believe that the reality of racism is too serious to risk dilution with socialism. When one reads the histories of black churches in the works of Joseph Washington, Carter G. Woodson, E. Franklin Frazier, Gayraud S. Wilmore[15] and others, it is revealing that there are no references to black socialist preachers.

The one event that presented the radical black church movement of the 1960s with an opportunity to consider the Marxist question was when James Forman issued *The Black Manifesto* in Riverside Church, May 4, 1969. While the National Conference of Black Churchmen supported Forman, their support ignored the Introduction of the *Manifesto* because it was Marxist. The black preachers of NCBC strongly endorsed the demands of the *Manifesto,* but sidestepped the Marxist justification of the demands, using instead their own nationalist arguments. While James Forman was referred to as a modern-day prophet by NCBC and other black church people, no black church person, to my knowledge, endorsed his perspective on Marxism. In fact, during all the discussion I attended on the *Manifesto* issue, no one even raised the issue of Marxism.

It was an intellectual failure on my part that I did not deal with Marxism and socialism in my early writings. But after encountering serious socialists who were also serious Christians in Africa, Asia, and Latin America, I began to reevaluate my silence on this theme. As a result I raised the socialism issue at the first black theology Conference in Atlanta, Georgia, August 1977, in a lecture entitled: "Black Theology and the Black Church: Where Do We Go From Here?"[16] Since that time, I have been convinced that the black church cannot remain silent regarding socialism, because such silence will be interpreted by our Third World brothers and sisters as support for the capitalistic system, which exploits the poor all over this earth.

For example, between twenty-five and fifty thousand people die each day from starvation as a result of national and international economic orders that foster distorted development. The former secretary of agriculture, Earl Butz, well known for his racial slurs, said it bluntly: "Food is a weapon. It is now one of the principle tools of our negotiating kit."[17] Sixty percent of the world's population are malnourished, 20 percent are starving, and one-third have less than three dollars per week on which to live. Never before has there been so much food production and also so much suffering from hunger. According to the United Nations Conference on Trade and Development's report in October 1976, the developed countries with 20 percent of the world's population have almost 67 percent of the world's income while the poorest 30 percent of humanity have only 3 percent of the world's income. It is little wonder that the nations of the world spend more than 500 billion annually on military weapons, over one-third of the total being spent in the United States. What is reflected in the international economic order in terms of the maldistribution of wealth is found also on the national scene in the United States. One percent of the people in the USA own 30 percent of the wealth.[18] From these economic realities, it ought to be clear that black churches cannot simply continue to ignore socialism as an alternative social arrangement. We cannot continue to speak against racism without any reference to a radical change in the economic order. I do not think that racism can be eliminated as long as capitalism remains intact. It is time for us to investigate socialism as an alternative to capitalism. One result will be to rediscover black socialist preachers, like George W. Woodbey, who were relegated to the periphery of the black church tradition because of their strong advocacy of socialism.

In addition to the prevailing attitude of indifference among Marxists and black church people, there have also been instances of hostility and mutual support. An example of the hostile attitude is found among the communists during the 1920s. One communist said of the black preacher: "The duty of the preacher is not alone to distract the mind of his congregation from their wretched conditions. It is also to serve the white plantation owners as their best agents in spying upon the activities of the rural populace. For so faithfully serving their masters, these lackeys often receive excellent wages."[19] This attitude continued until the early 1930s, when the communists began to change from hostility to support. They supported Father Divine and later Adam Clayton Powell, Jr. Powell said of the communists in 1945: "Today there is no group in America, including the Christian Church, that practices racial brotherhood one-tenth as much as the Communist Party."[20]

Because of their separate paths to radicalism and their mutual marginality in this society, Marxists and black church people continue their mutual misunderstanding, indifference, and hostility. As part of the present effort to move beyond massive neglect and occasional sniping, let us consider the unfavorable assumption by which Marxists and black church people have held each other at arm's length. I shall start with the black viewpoint and continue with the Marxist one, commenting on each point along the way.

The Black Church's View of Marxism

1. According to the black church, Marxist philosophy is atheistic and therefore must be rejected. How can the black church embrace a philosophy that denies God's existence, when the church is based on the faith that God will make a way out of no way? It appears that this fundamental objection would end dialogue before it begins.

However, the fact is that many people in Asia, Africa, and Latin America call themselves Marxists and Christians at the same time. They do so by distinguishing between Marxism as a world view (Weltanschauung) and Marxism as an instrument of social analysis, rejecting the former and enthusiastically taking up the latter. Black church people in this country may find themselves able to do the same thing. Marxism may be understood as a scientific tool for analyzing the economic, political, and social structures of this society so that we will know how to actualize in the world the freedom that we affirm in faith.

2. Blacks also observe that Marxism is European in origin and therefore white. Whiteness as such is of course no problem, but in the black experience whiteness almost always means racism. In the past, Marxists and other socialists have been predominantly racist by excluding blacks from their vision of the new socialist society. Some socialists advocated that blacks should be exported to Africa, and others claimed that their vision of a socialist society did not in any way eliminate racial segregation. Others, like Eugene Debs, one of the founders of the Socialist Party in the early twentieth century and a frequent Presidential candidate, remained ambivalent on the issue of racism. When the Socialist Party did take a stand against racism during the 1904 and 1908 conventions, the stand was weak and nothing was done to implement it. The party was concerned not to offend Southern white socialists who made it quite clear that there was a special place for black people and not even socialism could change that fact.

I think that blacks can overcome the problem of Marxism's being white and racist the same way we overcome the problem of Christianity being white and racist. We can indigenize Marxism, that is, reinterpret it for our situation. We do not refuse to ride in cars or airplanes, nor do we reject any other useful instruments just because they were invented by whites. Why then should we reject Marxism if it proves to be of use in our struggle for freedom?

3. Many white Marxists, especially the communists during the 1920s, referred to black preachers as ignorant and to their religion as superstition, a description that is not likely to win friends among black church people. My comment on this is that I am sure that white Christians, Democrats, and Republicans, have said and done worse things to us, and I do not hear black Christians saying that we should cease being Christians or reject Republicans and Democrats because some whites in these groups call us bad names.

4. When Marxists have been forced to face the question of race, they have always made it secondary to the economic question and the class struggle. While this may be scientifically correct, the way in which Marxists put forward their perspective on race and class is usually offensive to victims of racism. My personal encounter with white Marxists who emphasized that race is secondary and class is primary occurred in dialogues with Latin American liberation theologians and so-called white liberation theologians in North America. My response to that emphasis was to say: Even if that were true, no white person has the right to say it to a black person. People who do not suffer from a particular form of societal oppression have no right to tell people who do that their suffering is secondary and that the real struggle is located in another area. Furthermore when I think that it is the descendants of slave masters, the enslavers of my grandparents, who are saying such things, I get a little upset and wonder what kind of enslaving game is being planned for black people in the name of socialism.

The black church is a nationalist, race-oriented institution whose identity is inseparably connected with the struggle for freedom in this life as well as the eternal freedom believed to be coming in God's eschatological future. How then can the black church embrace a philosophy that by definition makes the elimination of racism secondary? This is a critical question, and its implications point to the heart of the conflict between the black church and Marxism. The question is whether the black church in particular and the black community generally have anything specific and unique to contribute to the struggle for liberation in this society. Marxists seem to deny that we have anything to contribute, and that is why they seldom turn to our tradition for insight and guidance. Like other whites, they seem to think that they have the whole, pure truth.

A Marxist View of the Black Church

1. According to Marxists, the black church preaches salvation as a reward to be received in heaven and not as justice on earth. In such a view, black religion serves the same function in the black community that religion serves in the white community. It is a sedative, an opiate that masks the pain of injustice on earth by directing people's attention toward the joy of heaven. Religion, according to Marxist doctrine, makes people depend wholly on God to change the world and leads them away from social analysis and from acting to create their own freedom. As Karl Marx said, "The more man puts into God, the less he retains in himself." It was in this context that Marx also described religion as "the *opium* of the people."[21]

As with the matter of atheistic ideology, the religion-sedative equation is part of the Marxist world view, which may be ignored while taking up Marxism as a tool of social analysis. To the Marxist claim that black religion is an opiate, we reply merely that sometimes it is and sometimes it is not.

Certainly the black church is not a consistent model of liberation. As long as we have the Reverend Ikes, we know that all is not well with what is known as black religion. However, the black church did define the gospel as liberation and did institutionalize its definition by creating separate, independent denominations in the early nineteenth century. We must not minimize the historical and theological importance of Richard Allen, Henry H. Garnett, David Walker, Henry M. Turner, and Martin Luther King, Jr., who with many others related the gospel to the black freedom struggle. When we speak of the black liberation struggle, we are talking about a movement that was created in and supported by the black church. We have always known that religion is political and the presence of white preachers as slaveholders and at the Klan rallies reinforced that fact within our theological consciousness. Accordingly many blacks have found in religion not an opiate but a tonic that gives courage and strength in the struggle for freedom.

2. Marxists often claim that when the black church does manage to come down to earth with its message of freedom, it focuses exclusively on racism as if that were the only problem with American society. It does not offer a critique of capitalism or seek to construct a completely new society. Such a limited vision, the Marxists claim, seems to suggest that the black church is a capitalist institution and its members are upset with American society only because they want a larger piece of the capitalistic pie. For the Marxist, the black church is reformist and not revolutionary.

Black church people need to take this critique seriously. We can say that in the history of our struggle, the oppression of black people was so extreme in every segment of our community that there was no opportunity for a comprehensive scientific analysis of American society, including a critique of capitalism and a consideration of socialism. Blacks were not a part of a European intellectual class but the descendants of African slaves. They simply responded to the most pressing contradiction in their historical experience, namely slavery and racism. They did not define their struggle as being against capitalism per se, and they did not recognize the need for a revolution as defined by Marxism. Blacks wanted to end racism as defined by slavery, lynching, and Jim Crow laws. Now, however, we have a small group of black intellectuals in the church and in other areas of black life who can provide the necessary leadership. They can and should offer black people a critique of capitalism and an alternative vision of social existence.

Where Do We Go From Here?

I would like to offer the following suggestions in order that the dialogue between the black church and Marxism might be deepened. Both Marxists and black church people must be open to hear what each is saying regarding their respective projects for justice. Without an openness from both sides, there is no way that a meaningful dialogue can occur.

The openness about which I speak must include on the part of Marxists a willingness to take seriously the uniqueness of black oppression in the world generally and the United States in particular. The uniqueness of black oppression is to be understood not theologically, as if blacks are elected by God, but only scientifically. It is a fact that most people who suffer in the world are people of color and not European. And it is a fact that the people responsible for that oppression are white Europeans. Marxists have to be open to hear the meaning of that fact by asking whether racism is embedded in the very history and structure of Western civilization. But Marxists and other socialists do not like to focus on their racism, and they try to make us blacks believe that racism will be automatically eliminated when capitalism is destroyed. In every European socialist society I have been in, including Cuba, the elimination of capitalism has not eliminated racism.

Marxists must further consider whether the black church has something distinctive to contribute to the struggle to create a new socialist society. Unless white socialists are willing to acknowledge our unique contribution to the struggle, then we have nothing to talk about. I will not participate in a dialogue with any group that assumes that their philosophy of social change is the only true one.

Another aspect of the openness about which I speak is the willingness of black church people to think about the total reconstruction of society along the lines of democratic socialism. We must be willing to recognize that a social arrangement based on the maximization of profit with little regard to the welfare of the people cannot be supported. Even "if modern marxism gives the wrong answers, at least it asks the right question."[22] Marxism is at least right in its critique of capitalism and in its affirmation of the class struggle. I do not believe that it is morally right for multinational corporations to have a monopoly on the ownership of the means of production of goods needed for human survival. The earth is the Lord's, and its resources are intended for all. No one has a right to control by private ownership the necessities of human life. If black churches do not take a stand against capitalism and for democratic socialism, for Karl Marx and against Adam Smith, for the poor in all colors and against the rich of all colors, for the workers and against the corporations, how can we expect socialists, Marxists, and other freedom fighters to believe us when we sing:

> Oh Freedom! Oh Freedom!
> Oh Freedom, I love thee!
> And before I'll be a slave,
> I'll be buried in my grave,
> And go home to my Lord and be free?

There cannot and should not be any serious dialogue between black churches and socialists if the former are unwilling to consider socialism as an alternative social arrangement.

Regardless of what happens in the dialogue between black churches and socialists, it is clear that we blacks must begin to think of a radical and total reconstruction of this society from its material, economic base. This reconstruction must include political freedom and racial and sexual equality—in short, the opportunity for all to become what we are meant to be. We must ask whether it is possible to end racism in a capitalistic society, whether a society based on the maximization of profit for a few corporate rich while the majority are dependent on wage-labor for survival can ever create freedom for black people. While a few "middle-class" blacks may benefit from the creation of a new intellectual and managerial class by corporations, we must ask about the masses of blacks—that 30 percent underclass, permanently unemployed, that 40 to 60 percent unemployed black youth, and a host of other blacks—who have little control over their survival. How do we propose to eliminate this extreme form of oppression? Can we deal effectively with our situation as oppressed blacks with the tactics used by our grandparents?

It is time for us to consider a radically new social arrangement.

The question is whether democratic socialism offers us such an alternative. Will it protect the freedoms we now enjoy and eliminate the evils that now exist? When the words "socialism" and "communism" are mentioned, most people think of Soviet Russia, Cuba, Eastern Europe, and other such places—all of which would be decisively rejected by democratic socialists as examples of "state capitalism." The problem with democratic socialism is that there are no historical models to which we can point in order to make our claims and goals concrete. White American capitalists often ask radical social critics, "Why don't you go somewhere else and live?" Or if they are more polite, they ask: "Where does such a socialist society exist, if the ones that adopt the name are not in fact socialist?"

These are hard questions, even if they do come from people who represent the consciousness of the ruling class. But I contend that the absence of a historical model should not deter us from our attempt to create one. For hope in black religion is based on a vision *not* present in, but created out of, historical struggle. If we limit our hope to what is, then we destroy hope. Hope is the expectation of that which is not. It is the belief that the impossible is possible, the "not yet" is coming in history. Without hope, the people perish. Hope is what enabled Frederick Douglass, Harriet Tubman, Rosa Parks, and Martin Luther King to actualize historical projects of freedom which others said were impossible. If we blacks today limit our hope to what is, that is, to the Democratic and Republican parties, then our vision is severely limited. If we define our struggle for freedom only within the alternatives posed by capitalism, then we have allowed our future humanity to be determined by what people have created and not by God. To believe in God is to know that our hope is grounded in Jesus Christ, the crucified Lord whose resurrected presence creates a new hope for a better world. Why not think that the "not yet" is possible? Why not think of a completely new society and begin to devise ways to realize it on earth. For if our heavenly visions have no earthly realizations, then they can only serve as a sedative that eases the pain of an unbearable present. Is that the extent of black religion's essence? Why are there no genuinely radical and independent voices coming from our leaders today? Why do they pose alternatives that exist only within capitalism, a system that offers no hope for the masses of blacks. Personally I like Andrew Young, the NAACP, the Urban League, the SCLC, Jesse Jackson, and our black elected officials, and I do not wish to minimize the hard work and devotion they have given on our behalf. The same is true for our ministers and theologians of the gospel. But what I find missing in what they propose is any genuinely new vision of the social order. Perhaps what we need today is to return to that "good old-time religion" of our grandparents and combine with it a Marxist critique of society. Together black religion and Marxist philosophy may show us the way to build a completely new society. With that combination, we may be able to realize in the society the freedom that we sing about and pray for in the black church.

Notes

Chapter 1. From Bearden to Adrian

1. See especially my *God of the Oppressed* (New York: Seabury, 1975), chapter 1; "Black Theology and the Black College Student" in *Journal of Afro-American Issues,* vol. 4, nos. 3 & 4, Summer/Fall 1976, pp. 420-31; "Gospel and the Liberation of the Poor" in *Christian Century,* February 18, 1981.

2. For Daisy Bates' account, see her *Long Shadow of Little Rock* (New York: David McKay Co., 1962).

3. Joseph Washington, *Black Religion* (Boston: Beacon Press, 1964). For accounts of the impact of this book on the rise of black theology, see my "Interpretation of the Debate Among Black Theologians" in Gayraud S. Wilmore and J. H. Cone, eds., *Black Theology: A Documentary History 1966-1979* (Maryknoll, N.Y.: Orbis Books, 1979), pp. 609-23; Wilmore, "Black Theology: Its Significance for Christian Mission Today," *International Review of Missions,* vol. 63, no. 250 (April 1974).

Chapter 2. Black Theology and Black Power

1. For the best account of the origin and development of NCBC, see Wilmore and Cone, eds., *Black Theology: A Documentary History 1966-1979,* parts I

and II (the Black Power statement of July 31, 1966, and other documents are included in this volume); G. S. Wilmore, *Black Religion and Black Radicalism* (Garden City, N.Y.: Doubleday, 1972), pp. 262-306; Leon Watts, "The National Committee of Black Churchmen" in *Christianity and Crisis,* vol. 30, no. 18 (November 1970), pp. 237-43.

2. The impact of Eric Lincoln upon my development as a theologian can hardly be overstated. Upon his suggestion, I sent my essay "Christianity and Black Power" to *The Christian Century* and *Motive,* but neither had space for it. When I told Lincoln, he then published a condensed version of it in his edited work, *Is Anybody Listening to Black America?* (New York: Seabury Press, 1968), pp. 3-9. It was my first publication.

3. See especially Ralph Ginzburg, *100 Years of Lynchings* (New York: Lancey Books, 1962).

4. James Forman's "Black Manifesto" is included in Wilmore and Cone, eds., *Black Theology: A Documentary History,* pp. 88-89.

5. NCBC's "Black Theology" statement is found in Wilmore and Cone, eds., *Black Theology: A Documentary History,* pp. 100-102.

6. Albert Cleage's best known work is his *Black Messiah* (New York: Sheed & Ward, 1968). See also his *Black Christian Nationalism* (New York: William Morrow, 1972).

7. For an official account of this meeting see Amiri Baraka/LeRoi Jones, ed., *African Congress: A Documentary of the First Modern Pan-African Congress* (New York: Morrow, 1972); see also Alex Poinsett, "It's Nation Time," in *Ebony,* vol. XXVI, no. 2, December 1970. For another account of my reactions to the Atlanta CAP meeting, see my "Black Theology and the College Student."

8. See "Dialogue on Black Theology," *Christian Century,* September 15, 1971, pp. 1079 ff.

9. (New York: Seabury Press, 1972.)

10. See his "Black Theology and Christian Theology" in Wilmore and Cone, eds., *Black Theology: A Documentary History,* pp. 144 ff. and his *Transfiguration of Politics* (New York: Harper, 1975).

11. For a broad range of responses of white theologians to black theology, see Wilmore and Cone, eds., *Black Theology: A Documentary History,* part III; and the *Union Seminary Quarterly Review,* Fall 1975.

12. Included in Wilmore and Cone, eds., *Black Theology: A Documentary History,* pp. 609-10. For black theologians' critique of my work, see Charles Long, "Perspectives for a Study of Afro-American Religion in the United States," *History of Religion,* August 1971; "Structural Similarities and Dissimilarities in Black and African Theologies," *Journal of Religious Thought,* Fall-Winter 1975; Wilmore, *Black Religion and Black Radicalism;* Cecil Cone, *Identity Crisis in Black Theology* (Nashville: AMEC, 1975).

13. (Philadelphia: Westminster Press, 1971.)

14. (Nashville: Abingdon Press, 1971.)

15. (Garden City, N.Y.: Doubleday, 1973.)

Chapter 3: Black Theology and the Black Church

1. The Richard Allen incident is well known. Bishop H. M. Turner's "God Is a Negro" was written in 1898 and is included in Edwin Redkey, ed., *Respect Black: The Writing and Speeches of Henry McNeal Turner* (New York: Arno Press, 1971).

2. The document that best explains my attraction BMCR is their "Black Paper, 1968," which was a part of a report of the Cincinnati meeting. It is reprinted in Wilmore and Cone, eds., *Black Theology: A Documentary History* pp. 268 ff.

3. See his *Church Dogmatics*, vol. I, part 1, trans. G. T. Thomson (Edinburgh: T. & T. Clark, 1936), pp. 98 ff.

4. Ibid., p. 104.

5. This paper was later published in *The Journal of the Interdenominational Center*, vol. IV, no. 1 (Fall 1977).

6. Monday, August 11, 1975.

7. Published in Wilmore and Cone, eds., *Black Theology: A Documentary History*, pp. 350-51.

8. Published in *The Journal of the Interdenominational Center*, vol. VII, no. 1 (Fall 1979).

Chapter 4. Black Theology and Third World Theologies

1. Most of the NCBC documents are included in Wilmore and Cone, eds., *Black Theology: A Documentary History*. The official account of the first formal consultation between black and African theologians and church people is Priscilla Massie, ed., *Black Faith and Black Solidarity* (New York: Friendship Press, 1973).

2. Regarding my writings on Third World theologies, see my "Black Theology: And Third World Theologies," in Wilmore and Cone, eds., *Black Theology: A Documentary History*, pp. 445-62. On African theology, see my (with Gayraud S. Wilmore) "Black Theology and African Theology: Considerations for Dialogue, Critique and Integration," in ibid., pp. 463-76; "Black and African Theologies: A Consultation," in *Christianity and Crisis*, March 3, 1975; "A Black American Perspective on the Future of African Theology," in *African Theology en Route*, ed. Kofi Appiah-Kubi and Sergio Torres (Maryknoll, N.Y.: Orbis Books, 1979), pp. 176-86. On Asian theology, see my "Black American Perspective on the Asian Search for Full Humanity," in Virginia Fabella, ed., *Asia's Struggle for Full Humanity* (Maryknoll, N.Y.: Orbis Books, 1980); "Asian Theology Today: Searching for Definitions," in *Christian Century*, May 23, 1979; "Asia's Struggle for a Full Humanity: Toward a Relevant Theology," in Wilmore and Cone, eds., *Black Theology: A Documentary History*, pp. 593-601. On Latin American theology, see my "From Geneva to Sao Paulo: A Dialogue Between Black Theology and Latin American Theology," in Sergio Torres and John

Eagleson, eds., *The Challenge of Basic Christian Communities* (Maryknoll, N.Y.: Orbis Books, 1981).

3. For one of the earliest texts on African theology, see Kwesi Dickson and Paul Ellingsworth, eds., *Biblical Revelation and African Beliefs* (London: Lutterworth, 1969).

4. One of the best introductions to Latin American liberation theology is Jose Miguez Bonino, *Doing Theology in a Revolutionary Situation* (Philadelphia: Fortress Press, 1975).

5. An introduction to Asian theology is found in Douglas J. Elwood, ed., *Asian Christian Theology: Emerging Themes* (Philadelphia: Westminster Press, 1980).

6. For the emerging emphasis of Caribbean theology, see Idris Hamid, ed., *Troubling of the Waters* (Trinidad: Ruhaman Printing, 1973).

7. For an introduction, see G. H. Anderson and T. F. Stransky, eds., *Mission Trends*, No. 4 (New York: Paulist Press, 1979).

8. Writings on feminist theology among whites are well known. For an emerging black feminist theology, see "Black Theology and Black Women," in Wilmore and Cone, eds., *Black Theology: A Documentary History*, part V, pp. 363-442.

9. See Sergio Torres and John Eagleson, eds., *Theology in the Americas* (Maryknoll, N.Y.: Orbis Books, 1976) for information on the origin of this organization. For information about Detroit II and the "Inter-Ethnic/Indigenous theologies Dialogue," see *Theology in the Americas: Detroit II Conference Papers*, eds. Cornel West, Caridad Guidote, and Margret Cookley (Maryknoll, N.Y.: Probe-Orbis Books, 1982) and the "Message from the Haudenosaunee Dialogue/Retreat," Native Self-Sufficiency Center, Theology in the Americas, 475 Riverside Drive, New York, N.Y. See also Gregory Baum, "Theology in the Americas: Detroit II," *The Ecumenist,* September-October 1980.

10. All the publications of our meetings of the Ecumenical Association of Third World Theologians have been published by Orbis Books in Maryknoll, N.Y. It should also be noted that plans are being made to hold conferences in the Caribbean and North America.

11. See John Mbiti, "An African Views American Black Theology," in Wilmore and Cone, eds., *Black Theology: A Documentary History,* pp. 477-78; Desmond Tutu, "Black Theology/African Theology," in ibid., pp 483-84; Monas Buthelezi, "An African Theology or a Black Theology," in *Black Theology: The South African Voice,* ed. Basil Moore (Atlanta: John Knox, 1973), pp. 29-30.

12. See especially Bonino's *Doing Theology in a Revolutionary Situation.*

Chapter 5. Black Theology, Feminism, and Marxism

1. "Double Jeopardy: To Be Black and Female" in Wilmore and Cone, eds., *Black Theology: A Documentary History,* p. 370.

2. Cited in Robert Staples, *The Black Woman in America: Sex, Marriage and the Family* (Chicago: Nelson-Hall, 1973), p. 69.

3. "Black Theology and the Black Woman," in Wilmore and Cone, eds., *Black Theology: A Documentary History*, p. 421.

4. Cited in Philip S. Foner, *American Socialism and Black Americans: From the Age of Jackson to World War II* (Westport, Conn.: Greenwood Press, 1977), p. 205.

5. Ibid., pp. 57, 59.

6. For an excellent analysis of Woodbey's perspective on socialism as well as other black socialist preachers, see ibid., chapter 7. See also Cornel West, "Black Theology and Marxist Thought" in Wilmore and Cone, *Black Theology: A Documentary History*, pp. 564-65. See also two additional essays by West, "Socialism and the Black Church," *New York Circus: A Center for Social Justice and International Awareness*, October-November 1979, vol. 3, no. 5, p. 508; and "Black Theology and Socialist Thought," *The Witness*, vol. 63, no. 4, April 1980, pp. 16-19.

7. (New York: Bantam, 1973.) See also Harrington, *Toward a Democratic Left: A Radical Program for a New Majority* (New York: Macmillan, 1968); *The Twilight of Capitalism* (New York: Touchstone, 1976).

8. (Princeton, N.J.: Princeton University Press, 1967.)

9. Weinstein, *The Decline of Socialism in America, 1912-1925* (New York: Vintage Books, 1969); see also his *Ambiguous Legacy: The Left in American Politics* (New York: New Viewpoints, 1975).

10. The invisibility of the black radicals in the writings of writers on the left is also found in Peter Clecak's *Radical Paradoxes: Dilemmas of the American Left: 1945-1970* (New York: Harper Torchbooks, 1974); T. B. Bottomore, *Critics of Society: Radical Thought in North America* (New York: Vintage Books, 1969). In the 1968 revision of this book, first published in 1966, there is added a "Postscript," and it covers Bottomore's interpretation of the civil rights and Black Power movements. Christopher Lasch, *The New Radicalism in America: 1889-1963* (New York: Vintage Books, 1965) is also conspicuous for its absence of any references to black radicalism. However, in his *Agony of the American Left* (New York: Vintage Books, 1969), there is a penetrating analysis of "Black Power: Cultural Nationalism as Politics." But even here, he is silent on earlier black radicals in the black church and other segments of black life.

11. See also Robert L. Allen (with the collaboration of Pamela P. Allen), *Reluctant Reformers: Racism and Social Reform Movements in the United States* (Garden City, N.Y.: Doubleday, 1975). The most perceptive critic of the white left is Harold Cruse. See his *The Crisis of the Negro Intellectual* (New York: Morrow, 1967); and *Rebellion or Revolution* (New York: Morrow, 1968).

12. Cited in Daniel Bell, *Marxian Socialism in the United States* (Princeton: Princeton University Press, 1952), p. 36.

13. Cited in Foner, *American Socialism and Black Americans*, p. 219.

14. Cited in ibid., p. 85. Foner's treatment of black socialist preachers in chapter

7 of this volume is excellent. Other articles by black socialist preachers include Bishop James T. Holly's "Socialism From the Biblical Point of View," *The AME Church Review*, vol. 10, 1894; George F. Miller, "Enslavement and Its Ethical Basis," *The Messenger*, vol. II, no. 7, July 1919. I am especially appreciative to my colleague, Professor James Washington, for sharing copies of the Holly and Miller articles with me.

15. Joseph Washington, *Black Religion: The Negro and Christianity in the United States* (Boston: Beacon Press, 1964); Carter G. Woodson, *The History of the Negro Church* (Washington, D.C.: Associated Publishers, 1972); E. Franklin Frazier, *The Negro Church in America* (New York: Schocken Books, 1962); Gayraud S. Wilmore, *Black Religion and Black Radicalism* (Garden City, N.Y.: Doubleday, 1973).

16. This essay is included in Wilmore and Cone, eds., *Black Theology: A Documentary History*, pp. 350-59.

17. See *Christianity and Crisis*, January 24, 1977. The current secretary of agriculture, John R. Block, has made similar remarks.

18. See G. William Domhoff, *The Powers That Be: Processes of Ruling Class Domination in America* (New York: Vintage Books, 1979); see also his *Who Rules America* (Englewood Cliffs, N.J.: Prentice-Hall, 1967).

19. Cited in Ralph L. Roy, *Communism and the Churches* (New York: Harcourt, Brace, 1960), p. 48.

20. Adam C. Powell, Jr., *Marching Blacks* (New York: Dial Press, 1973), p. 67. Originally published in 1945.

21. *The Marx-Engels Reader*, ed. Robert C. Tucker (New York: W. W. Norton; 2nd ed., 1978), pp. 72, 54.

22. A comment by Denys Munby cited in J. Philip Wogaman, *The Great Economic Debate: An Ethical Analysis* (Philadelphia: Westminster Press, 1977), p. 55.